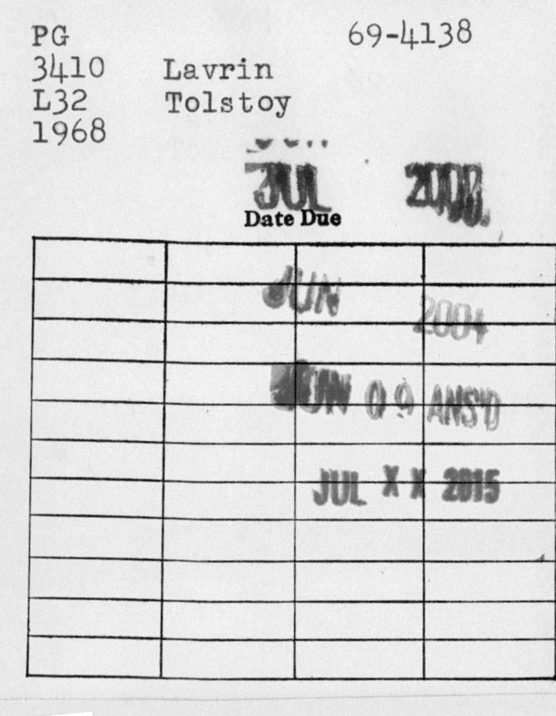

TOLSTOY

By courtesy of The Society for Cultural Relations with the U.S.S.R.

LEO TOLSTOY IN 1910

TOLSTOY

AN APPROACH

BY

JANKO LAVRIN

NEW YORK / RUSSELL & RUSSELL

REISSUED, 1968, BY RUSSELL & RUSSELL
A DIVISION OF ATHENEUM PUBLISHERS, INC.
BY ARRANGEMENT WITH JANKO LAVRIN
L. C. CATALOG CARD NO: 68-27072
PRINTED IN THE UNITED STATES OF AMERICA

Note

THIS book is not a biography, but an attempt to interpret Tolstoy the man, the artist, and the thinker in the light of some of our present-day needs and problems. Although based on one of my previous studies of Tolstoy, this 'approach' contains a certain amount of new material some of which became available only fairly recently.

As for quotations, they are taken from the *Tolstoy Centenary Edition,* translated by Mr. and Mrs. Aylmer Maude (Humphrey Milford), and from *The Complete Works of Count Leo Tolstoy,* edited and translated by Dr. Leo Wiener (Dent). I also made use of a few quotations from the following works: *Leo Tolstoy,* by P. Biryukov (Heinemann); *The Life of Tolstoy,* by Aylmer Maude (Constable); *The Diaries of Tolstoy* (Dent); *The Journals of Tolstoy* (Knopf); *The Diary of Tolstoy's Wife,* and *The Countess Tolstoy's Later Diary,* both translated by Alexander Werth (Gollancz); *Tolstoy's Love Letters; Reminiscences of Tolstoy by Gorky; The Autobiography of Countess Tolstaya; Talks with Tolstoy,* by A. B. Goldenveizer. These last four books were published by the Hogarth Press. In the case of *Christianity and Patriotism* (Cape) I used Mrs. Constance Garnett's translation.

Facts referring to the last phase of Tolstoy's life are partly illustrated by quotations from S. A. Tolstaya's *The Final Struggle*—with the parallel extracts from Tolstoy's diaries—translated by Aylmer Maude (Unwin). To the publishers and translators of the mentioned works my thanks and acknowledgments are due. Translations of several passages from Tolstoy's letters and diaries are my own.

J. L.

Contents

CHAPTER		PAGE
	NOTE	v
I.	SOME GENERAL REMARKS	1
II.	THE ART OF TOLSTOY (I)	19
III.	THE ART OF TOLSTOY (II)	35
IV.	TOLSTOY'S DILEMMA	50
V.	CULTURE AND NATURE	67
VI.	THE 'DRAGON OF DEATH'	81
VII.	TOLSTOY AND RELIGION	93
VIII.	THE MILLENNIUM	104
IX.	A PURITAN'S PROGRESS	116
X.	THE LAST ACT	131
XI.	TOLSTOY AND THE REVOLUTION	143
XII.	TOLSTOY AND NIETZSCHE	153
	CONCLUSION	162
	INDEX	165

TOLSTOY

I

Some General Remarks

LEO NIKOLAYEVITCH TOLSTOY is one of the few authors of the last century whose greatness is no longer questioned. Having stood the test of time, he is now among the world-classics. His art has proved strong and vital enough not only to defy, but also to ignore the whims of literary fashions. This does not mean that Tolstoy the prophet and the guide in matters of the spirit is of the same importance as Tolstoy the artist. Yet only by clarifying, as far as possible, the relationship between the two, can we perhaps obtain an idea of the essential Tolstoy, and of what is truly valuable in him and his work. In this task we are no longer hampered by Tolstoy the myth or the legend. The generation which was able to watch the last years of Tolstoy's life could not help being affected by the wellnigh legendary aura emanating from that figure. From afar, at any rate, he looked like a mysterious (and often mystifying) giant, entitled by nature itself to judge, to value, to approve or to condemn. The more so because he actually commanded universal attention. An epoch which was rapidly losing its moral, social, and political responsibility, was quite willing to label Tolstoy as a sage and even to regard him as the 'conscience of Europe'—in order to continue its own nefarious dealings with the same lack of conscience as before. But for this very reason it was primarily Tolstoy the *legend* with whom millions of people became familiar. They were vaguely puzzled by the famous Russian Count who suddenly denounced his wealth, his class, even his artistic genius, and, having donned a peasant's garb, wanted to distribute his property among the poor. And what commotion was caused, from one end of the earth to the other, during his tragic flight and death, at the age of eighty-two! There certainly was plenty of material to give the name of Tolstoy not only a dramatic but also a sensational flavour which need, however, no longer trouble us in our study of his personality and work.

The story of Tolstoy's life is so well known that we can limit ourselves only to those essential facts which, in some way or other, help us to understand his work as a whole. Born in 1828 at Yasnaya Polyana into a family of rural aristocrats, he spent his early years in the comfortable and leisurely atmosphere of that class. It was against the background of the beautiful landscape of central Russia that he formed his first notions of the world in which he lived. These were provided not only by the people of his own social standing, but also by the patriarchal peasantry with its variety of types: toilers rooted in the land they worked, household servants, pilgrims, story-tellers, and even half-crazy simpletons in Christ—such as Grisha, described in his *Childhood*. His mother (*née* Princess Marie Volkonskaya) died when he was barely eighteen months old. At the age of nine he lost his father. The fact that he did not know his mother left the stamp of severity and diffidence in him. It may have been responsible also for certain peculiarities in his later attitude towards sex. Fortunately, one of his distant relatives, Tatyana Yergolskaya, took care of him, of his three elder brothers, and of his sister Maria. Later, Tolstoy gave a portrait of his 'aunty' Tatyana as the gently submissive Sonya in *War and Peace*. In his autobiographic reminiscences he stressed, moreover, the influence she had had on his life. 'This influence,' he says, 'consisted first in that ever since childhood she taught me the spiritual delight of love. She taught me this, but not in words: by her whole being she filled me with love. I saw, I felt how she enjoyed loving, and I understood the joy of love.' Even some of the games which he and his three brothers played as children were tinged with that desire for universal happiness and love which was to become the *leitmotif* of so many of his writings.

In the same reminiscences Tolstoy disclosed other characteristics, typical of him as a child. The joyful, almost ecstatic awareness of his own body was one of them. This is how he described the earliest impression he remembered: 'I am sitting in a wooden trough and am enveloped by the new and not unpleasant smell of some kind of stuff with which my little body is being rubbed. It was probably bran, and most likely I was having a bath; but the novelty of the bath aroused me, and for the first time I remarked and liked my little body with the ribs showing on the breast, and the smooth, dark-coloured trough, my nurse's rolled-up sleeves and the warm steaming bran-water, and its sound; and especially the feeling of the smoothness of the trough's edges when I passed my little hands along them.'

These few lines are the earliest reflection of Tolstoy's joy in things corporeal, in things affecting his body and its senses. Yet another marked feature began to assert itself very early: his awareness and censure of what, from his own standpoint, was 'not right'. In the same account of his childhood he describes a roundelay in which he and his German tutor, Theodor Ivanovitch,[1] took part. 'Among us there were women, strangers to us, and we all began to circle round and jump; and Theodor Ivanovitch jumped, lifting his legs too high, flinging about and making a great noise. And I felt at one and the same moment that this was not right, and that it was wicked, and I rebuked him, and I think I began to cry, and everything ceased.' Does not this passage anticipate, as it were, Tolstoy the moralist who, fifty years later, kept on rebuking the whole world for the things he regarded as

[1] The Russians never call each other by family name, but by Christian name and patronymic. This rule is applied also to foreigners living in Russia.

wicked, and was anxious that all the joy of life should cease?

Even Tolstoy's hatred of violence and authority can be traced back to some of his early experiences. On one occasion, when his French tutor St. Thomas locked him up and by way of punishment, threatened to flog him, he reacted with anger and indignation of which he himself says: 'Very likely this incident was the cause of the dreadful horror and repulsion towards every kind of violence which I have experienced all my life.' Another characteristic of Tolstoy the boy was his propensity to put every striking idea and desire into practice, regardless of whether it was feasible or not. At the age of eight he had an irresistible wish to fly by sitting on his heels and clasping his arms round his knees. When he actually tried to fly away from the high window-sill, he fell to the ground where he was found unconscious, with a slight concussion of the brain. In his *Boyhood* he tells us how once the thought occurred to him that happiness depends not so much on external conditions as on our personal attitude towards them. So he immediately wanted to become accustomed to suffering: now by holding in his outstretched hand a heavy volume of the Encyclopaedia for five minutes, then by whipping his back so severely that tears sprang to his eyes. On another occasion again the idea that death was preying upon him all the time overcame him so powerfully that he refused to understand how people had failed hitherto to enjoy each passing moment, before everything was snatched away by death. As a result, he at once gave up his lessons and for three days did nothing but lie on the bed, reading romances and eating gingerbread with honey.

Tolstoy's eccentric character must have been notably influenced also by his unattractive exterior. This tended to make him self-conscious and shy. But at the same time it fostered his pride, vanity, and secret ambitions, partly as a compensation and partly as a safety-valve against his own feeling of inferiority. 'I fancied', he says in *Childhood,* 'that there was no happiness on earth for a person with such a wide nose, such thick lips, and such small grey eyes as I had. I besought God to work a miracle, to turn me into a beauty, and all I had in the present, or might have in the future, I would give in exchange for a handsome face.' And in *Boyhood*: 'I was modest by nature, but my modesty was further increased by my own ugliness. And I am sure that nothing has such a decisive influence upon a man's course as his personal appearance, and not so much his appearance as his belief in its attractiveness. I was too egotistical to become accustomed to my position, and consoled myself, like the fox, by assuring myself that the grapes were still green; that is to say, I endeavoured to despise all the pleasures derived from the pleasing exterior which Volodya[1] enjoyed in my eyes, and which I envied with all my soul, and I strained every nerve of my mind and imagination to find solace in proud solitude.'

The fact that he started dissecting himself in his diaries at a very early age is a further proof of his egotism. In his 'proud solitude' he often refused to attach any importance to things and ideas, except to those which concerned him and in which he himself was engrossed. This made him indifferent or else intolerant to other people's opinions, whereas his own ideas assumed a significance quite out of proportion with their intrinsic value simply because they were his own. But this itself was a sign of his hidden doubts. Only a person anxious to conceal his uncertainty and to overcome his own vacillation, will barricade himself behind that protective egotism which Tolstoy eventually defined in the following sentence, written in a letter to his friend and distant relative Countess Alexandra Tolstaya (in 1874). 'Whatever I do I always try to convince myself that *de haut de ces pyramides*

[1] The names and certain external data (those about his parents, for instance) may not be reliable in that transposed autobiography, yet all the psychological data are invariably true.

40 *siècles me contemplent,* and that the whole world will perish if I stop.'

Nor should we overlook the potential inner complexity even in Tolstoy the boy. Judging by his own confession in *Boyhood,* he was not a stranger, even at a tender age, to certain 'dark' moods, the checking of which demanded both moral and mental self-control. 'In recalling my boyhood', he writes, 'I very clearly appreciate the importance of the most frightful crime, committed without object or intent to injure, but from curiosity, to meet an unconscious need of activity. There are moments when the future presents itself to a man in such sombre colours, that he dreads to fix his mental gaze upon it, entirely represses the action of his mind, and endeavours to convince himself that the future will not be, and the past has not been. At such moments, when thought does not sit in judgment of every decision of the will, and the fleshly instincts remain the sole spring of life, I can understand how a child is especially inclined to set and light a fire under the very house in which his brothers, his father, and his mother, whom he tenderly loves, are sleeping, without the slightest hesitation or fear, and with a smile of curiosity. Under the influence of this temporary absence of reflection, approaching aberration of mind, a peasant lad of seventeen, contemplating the freshly sharpened edge of an axe, gazes with stupid curiosity at the blood, as it drips from the severed neck on the bench; under the influence of the same absence of reflection and instinctive curiosity, a man experiences a certain enjoyment in pausing upon the brink of a precipice, and thinking, "What if I should throw myself down here?" Or, placing a loaded pistol to his forehead, he thinks, "What if I pull the trigger?" Or he gazes upon some person for whom society universally cherishes a peculiar respect, and thinks, "What if I were to go up to him, take him by the nose, and say: 'Come, my dear fellow, shall we go?' " ' One can well imagine why Tolstoy gradually felt the need of attaching more and more importance to logical reflection, or to 'thought sitting in judgment of every decision of the will'.

From these early reminiscences and avowals one can derive practically the entire character of the grown-up Tolstoy. They shed a light on the inner contradictions from which he suffered and with which he had to contend to the end of his days. Spontaneous joy in existence and an intolerant moral campaign against it; an incredibly acute realism in art, and a complete lack of it in his theories; hatred of all authority, and at the same time a tendency to impose an authoritative strait-jacket on all human instincts—such were some of those contradictions.

II

Tolstoy left Yasnaya Polyana first for Moscow and then for Kazan, where he entered the University. In 1849 he gave up his University studies as a failure and settled down on his estate with all sorts of reformatory plans and projects. After a brief and hardly successful stay in the country (recorded in his unfinished story, *A Landowner's Morning*), he left for the Caucasus and joined, for a couple of years, the Caucasian Cossacks. He hunted with them, caroused, fought against the rebellious mountaineers, and seemed quite pleased with his new companions, whom he recorded in his novel, *The Cossacks* (written in 1852, but published ten years later). He was fascinated not only by the spontaneity, but also by the wholeness of those primitive children of Nature—the wholeness which was denied to him, however much he may have longed for it.

It was typical of Tolstoy that even at his most spontaneous moments his introspection and self-analysis always lay in wait for him—a quality which is more than apparent in *The Cossacks*. It is equally conspicuous in the diaries he wrote, from his University years in Kazan onwards. The most radical overhaul he made of himself is recorded, however, in the entry dated July 7th, 1854, that is, when he had already left the Caucasus in order to take part in the Crimean campaign. 'I have no modesty,' he says there. 'This is my great deficiency. What am I? One of the four sons of a retired lieutenant-colonel, left from the age of seven without parents, and who, under the guardianship of women and strangers, received neither a worldly nor scientific education, and then became emancipated at seventeen; a man without any great wealth, without any social position and, above all, without principles, who has let his affairs get out of order to the last extremity, who has passed the best years of his life without aim or pleasure; who finally banished himself to the Caucasus in order to run away from his debts and, above all, from his habits, and who, having taken advantage of some connexion or other which had existed between his father and a commander-in-chief, has got himself transferred, at the age of twenty-six, to the army of the Danube as a lieutenant, with hardly any means but his pay (having to use such means as he possesses for the payment of his remaining debts), without patrons, without knowledge of worldly matters, without knowledge of the service, without practical capacities, but with enormous vanity. Yes, such is my social position. Let us see what is my personality. I am ugly, awkward, uncleanly, and, in the worldly sense, uneducated; I am irritable, a bore to others, rude, intolerant, and as bashful as a child. I am almost completely ignorant. What I do know I have learned anyhow, independently, by snatches, incoherently, in a disorderly way, and all comes to—so little. I am self-indulgent, irresolute, inconstant, stupidly vain and hotheaded, as are all people with a weak character. I am not brave, I am not methodical in my life, and am so lazy that for me idleness has become almost a necessary habit. I am intelligent, but my intelligence has not yet been thoroughly tried on anything. I have neither a practical nor a worldly nor a business intelligence. I am honest, i.e. I love what is right, have got myself into the habit of loving it; and when I deviate from it I am dissatisfied with myself, and return to it with pleasure, but there are things I like more than what is right—fame. I am so vain, and so little has this feeling been gratified in me that often I am afraid lest, between fame and virtue, I might, if the choice were given me, choose the former. Yes, I am arrogant, because I am inwardly proud, though I am shy in society.'

While still in the Caucasus, Tolstoy wrote his *Childhood*. The work appeared in *The Contemporary* (in 1852) and was hailed as a valuable contribution to Russian fiction. Tolstoy's second success was his series of three Sebastopol stories (1854–5), based on personal experiences and observations during the Crimean campaign. After the campaign Tolstoy left the army and led, for a while, a rather dissipated existence in the Russian capital. He was particularly reckless at gambling—not unlike Dostoevsky. His literary fame gave him access to *The Contemporary* circle, which included the most distinguished authors of that period. But Tolstoy was not popular among them. Whatever his virtues, consideration of others was not one of them. Intolerant with regard to any views which differed from his own, he always wanted to have the last word. He was most self-assertive in his arguments with Turgenev, whom he treated as though vacillating all the time between spiteful jealousy and secret admiration.

Turgenev himself once referred to him as a troglodyte, and probably not without reason. A typical row between the two was recorded by Tolstoy's friend, the poet A. A. Fet, from the words of the author D. V. Grigorovitch who was present when it took place. It all happened at the poet Nekrasov's (the editor of *The Contemporary*), and this is what the scene was like when the argument came to a head. 'Turgenev speaks more and more shrilly, then pressing his hand to his throat, and with a look of a dying gazelle, whispers: "I cannot talk any longer! It will give me bronchitis!"

And with enormous strides begins to walk up and down the three rooms. "Bronchitis!" sneers Tolstoy. "It's an imaginary illness. Bronchitis is a metal!" Of course the host Nekrasov is trembling heart and soul: he is afraid to lose both Turgenev and Tolstoy, in whom he foresees a powerful support for *The Contemporary,* so he is bound to manœuvre. We are all upset and at a loss what to say. Tolstoy is lying down in the middle of the room on a leather sofa and sulking; Turgenev with the lapels of his jacket asunder and his hands in his pockets, continues to walk up and down all the three rooms. To prevent a catastrophe, I approached the sofa and said: "My dear Tolstoy, don't get excited! You have no idea how he appreciates and likes you!" "I will not allow him," says Tolstoy, his nostrils dilating, "to be spiteful to me. And now he walks up and down the room on purpose, wagging his democratic tail before me." ' The animosity between the two authors reached, later on, such a pitch that Tolstoy challenged Turgenev to a duel. The duel did not take place, but the differences were not patched up for years. Turgenev, who showed more generosity and goodwill than his younger literary rival, defined a few years after (in a letter to Fet on January 7th, 1862) his attitude to Tolstoy as follows: 'I like him very much at a distance, I respect him and watch his career with sympathy, but when we come together everything takes a different aspect. It cannot be helped! We must go on living as if we existed on different planets or in different ages.'

Shy and conscious of his own defects, Tolstoy was intolerant simply in order to guard his own independence in the presence of others. If he said that bronchitis was a metal, then it had to be a metal, and that was the end of it. According to reliable witnesses, he often carried (and with evident pleasure) his whims and opinions to such lengths as to contradict everybody around for the sake of mere contradiction. 'Whatever judgment might have been passed and the greater the authority of his interlocutor, the more he would insist on asserting the opposite view in as sharp terms as possible. Watching how he listened to his opponent, how he scrutinized him, how sarcastically he curled his lips, one would have thought he was concerned not so much with answering a question as with expressing an opinion which would both puzzle and surprise his questioner. In discussion he used to push his argument to the farthest extreme.'

Such was the impression the young Tolstoy had made on Grigorovitch. And this is what, several decades later, Tolstoy himself wrote to his own biographer P. Biryukov: 'A trait of my character, it may be good or ill, but one which was always peculiar to me, is that in spite of myself I always used to resist epidemic influences. . . I had a hatred of the general tendency.' His natural inclination drove him, moreover, to the farthest extremes not only in arguments, but also in life. He acknowledged that much in a letter (November 2nd, 1856) to Valerie Arsenev—the first woman whom he intended to marry. 'I stake everything on one throw,' he says. 'If I do not find complete happiness, then I shall ruin everything, my talent, my heart; I shall become a drunkard, a gambler, provided I have not enough courage to cut my own throat. . . . I can't help it, but I am like that, and I neither conceal nor exaggerate it. Think it over if you can love such a monster.'

More successful in literature than in love, Tolstoy worked upon several stories, including *Youth* (1857) which is a sequel to his *Childhood* and *Boyhood*. In 1857 and again in 1860–61, he travelled abroad, where he met the Utopian socialist Proudhon, the German author Auerbach (known by his stories from peasant life), and the Russian revolutionary Alexander Herzen. Amongst other things, he witnessed a public execution in France, and the death of his brother Nicholas at Hyères—two events which left a profound scar on his inner life. Generally speaking, Tolstoy was even less favourably impressed by the one-sided trend of Western civilization than Herzen before him, or Dostoevsky whose first acquaintanceship with Western Europe dates from the same period. The defiant story *Luzern* (1857) testifies to some of Tolstoy's immediate reactions. Different in pattern and character are his *Family Happiness* (1859) and *Polikushka* (1861). The first is a short novel, told in the first person by the heroine and evidently reflecting Tolstoy's own dreams about Valerie Arsenev, with whom he had parted some three years earlier. The second story, on the other hand, is at least externally connected with the pathetic narratives about serfs, introduced into Russian literature by Grigorovitch. But the representatives of German populism, such as Gotthelf and Auerbach, may also have had something to do with it.

It is significant that about the same time Tolstoy began to look for an outlet in direct educational work by opening a school for peasant children on his estate. In 1859 he intimated to his friend Chicherin that he even intended to give up his literary occupations, on the ground that 'self-deception of the so-called artists is, on the part of those who submit to it, the most abominable baseness and lie'. The only alternative to literature could have been of course some practical and 'useful' activity—quite in the spirit of the utilitarian 'sixties. No wonder he was active as a teacher in 1859, and especially in the winter 1861–2, all the time doing his very best to refute the 'general tendency' in education. In February 1862 he even started the short-lived periodical, *Yasnaya Polyana,* in which he expounded his own educational principles. Basically, they differed little from Rousseau but for his intense populism. Regarding the uneducated ordinary people as the salt of the earth, as something naturally good, he advocated that the intellectuals should learn from the people, and not vice versa. Otherwise his chief educational aim was to promote equality, brotherhood, and moral progress among men. His wish to shape life not only in fiction, but also in reality was so strong indeed that even later, after having reached the summit of literary fame in Russia, he could not resist compiling a model ABC book for school-children (1872). Another trait, strongly noticeable in his periodical, was his attitude to civilization, which was even more negative than that of Rousseau.

After his marriage to Sophia Andreyevna Behrs, in 1862, he quietened down for a few years. His practical wife did all she could to enable him to create in comfort works of a wider range and scope than before. As though refreshed by his school activities, he decided, in 1863, to start a novel about the Decembrists.[1] While collecting the materials he found it necessary first to tackle, in the way of an introduction, the preceding period—the period of Napoleon's campaigns and the invasion of Russia in 1812. But the supposed introduction itself resulted in *War and Peace,* one of the greatest novels ever written. Concluded in 1869, it was followed, in 1875–7, by *Anna Karenina.* These two masterpieces brought Tolstoy universal fame and recognition. Yet when praise and honours were showered upon him, he rejected them with proud humility: as though fame itself was something he could now afford to laugh at and to despise. Soon he began to decry the very art to which he owed his fame, and shifted his attention to 'ultimate things'. A conversion followed and, together with it, a new outlook upon both art and life.

'At first I experienced moments of perplexity and arrest of life, as though I did not know how to live and what to do,' he says in his *Confession* (1879) of the few years preceding his conversion, 'and I felt lost, and became dejected. But this passed, and I went on living as before. Then these moments of perplexity began to recur oftener and oftener, and always in the same form: What is it for? What does it lead to? I felt that what I had been standing on had broken down, and that

[1] The name of those aristocratic liberals who, on December 14th, 1825, raised a revolt against the new emperor Nicholas I. The revolt was suppressed. Five of the ringleaders were executed and the rest were sent to Siberia.

I had nothing left under my feet. What I had lived by no longer existed, and I had nothing to live by. My life came to a standstill, I could breathe, eat, drink, and sleep, and I could not help doing these things; but there was no life, for there were no wishes the fulfilment of which I considered reasonable. . . . Had a fairy come and offered to fulfil my desires I should not have known what to ask. . . . If in a moment of intoxication I felt something which I cannot call a wish, but a habit left by former wishes, in sober moments I knew this to be a delusion, and that there is really nothing to wish for, I could not even wish to know the truth, for I guessed in what it consisted. The truth was that life was meaningless. . . . I could give no reasonable meaning to any single action, or to my whole life. I was only surprised that I could have avoided understanding this from the very beginning—it has been so long known to all. To-day or to-morrow sickness or death will come to those I love, or to me; nothing will remain but stench and worms. Sooner or later my affairs, whatever they may be, will be forgotten, and I shall not exist. Then why go on making any effort? . . . One can only live while one is intoxicated with life; as soon as one is sober it is impossible not to see that it is all mere fraud and stupid fraud! That is precisely what it is: there is nothing either amusing or witty about it: it is simply cruel and stupid.'

III

It was Tolstoy's sudden rupture with art and with his former 'senseless' existence—a rupture most poignantly described in his *Confession,* that fixed on him the attention of the world at large. The world saw in it above all a pretext for puzzled gossip, hardly suspecting the long and painful process which made Tolstoy take such a step. Not self-expression through art, but moral self-perfection became, from now on, his principal aim and gospel. The didactic teacher and denier of civilization emerged in him once again, but more potently and on a new plane. Turgenev, who visited Tolstoy in 1880, wrote of him as follows: 'It is an unpardonable sin that Leo Tolstoy has stopped writing. . . . Such an artist, such a first-rate talent we have never had nor now have among us. I, for instance, am considered an artist, but what am I as compared with him! In contemporary European literature he has no equal. Whatever he takes up, it all becomes alive under his pen. And how wide the sphere of his creative power—it is simply amazing! But what is one to do with him? He has plunged headlong into another sphere: has surrounded himself with Bibles and Gospels in nearly all languages, and has written a heap of papers. He has a trunk full of these mystical ethics and pseudo-interpretations. He read to me some extracts which I simply don't understand. I told him that something was wrong with all that. "It's just the right thing," he replied. . . . Most likely, he will give nothing more to literature; or if he reappears, it will be with that trunk.'

Turgenev was only partly right. For a while, at any rate, Tolstoy concentrated on all sorts of religious, moral, and theological pamphlets at the expense of any other writings. A year after his *Confession,* he finished his *Criticism of Dogmatic Theology* in which he attacked official Christianity. In *What I believe* (1884) he brought his own interpretation of Christ's message into a system. The same views were repeated and expanded by him in *What Then Must We Do* (1886), *On Life* (1887), *The Kingdom of God Is Within You* (1893), and *What Is Religion* (1902), to mention only the principal works of this kind. His aesthetic and his moral sense now became definitely divorced, and the latter won the battle. The ominous 'trunk', mentioned in Turgenev's letter, began to weigh heavy indeed. Yet it failed to crush the artist in Tolstoy. Even after his conversion some further masterpieces came from his pen. That terrifying narrative, *The Death of Ivan Ilyitch* (1886), was one of them. The peasant drama, *The Power of Darkness* (1886), was another. There followed such splendid stories as *Master and Man* (1895), *Father Sergius* (1898), *Hadji Murad* (1901–4), *The False Coupon* (1903–5), and also his last long novel, *Resurrection* (1899).

True enough, with few exceptions, the pressure of the 'trunk' remained. Even Tolstoy's best works now bore the stamp of his message in the name of which he denounced everything that did not agree with it, and this meant pretty well the whole of life. His frankness and fearless daring were so great as to impress the world. His indictments often hit the mark even when the remedies offered by him were doubtful and unconvincing. Conscious of his new role, Tolstoy jotted down in his diary in 1899: 'I am all the time the same man, but now I am the public, and then the judge himself with the chain, fulfilling the highest responsibilities. One must put on the chain more often.'

IV

He made ample use of the chain. His voice became so compelling at times that the eyes of the best Europeans (and not only Europeans) kept on turning towards Yasnaya Polyana, in the expectation of the craved for 'new word'. Yet for some reason or other that word did not turn up. Even a number of those people who were less acute than Turgenev could not help feeling a flaw in Tolstoy the prophet, however much they admired Tolstoy the artist. Besides, he himself gave many a proof that underneath his prophetic garb there remained the same lacerated, restless, and painfully seeking soul as before, in spite of his preaching and his assertions that he had discovered the secret of happiness for all. It was the aged Tolstoy, blessed with literary fame and the halo of a moral teacher, who once confessed to Gorky: 'The Kaliph Abdurahman had during his life fourteen happy days, but I am sure I have not had so many. And this is because I have never lived—I cannot live—for myself, for my own self; I live for show, for people.' Already in 1897 the same Tolstoy intended retiring from the world, not because he had found inner peace and harmony, but because he hoped to find them. 'Just as Hindoos, nearing sixty, retire into the woods, and as old religious men seek to devote their last years to God and not to jokes, puns, gossip, or tennis, so for me, entering my seventieth year the desire which absorbs my whole soul is for tranquillity, solitude, and, *if not for entire harmony,*[1] then at least for avoiding the crying discord between my life on the one hand, and my belief and conscience on the other.'

There is much evidence that Tolstoy's old age was not one of harmony, or even peace. At the height of worldly fame he felt perhaps lonelier than ever. Although unable to follow his own Christian principles to the letter, he did what he could to live up to them under the circumstances which were stronger than his will or his character. Yet on March 5th, 1901, he was excommunicated by the Holy Synod as an anti-Christian. Dissensions kept on growing also between him and his wife who admired her husband's literary genius, but —for sensible reasons of her own—repudiated, and most decisively so, his teaching and preaching. Nor was there much love lost between her and the odd collection of Tolstoyan cranks and pilgrims streaming to their teacher's feet. It was in their midst in particular that Tolstoy was almost compelled to 'live for show, for people'. For one thing, he often had to pretend to be as simple as his worshippers, in order not to disappoint them. So even the more intelligent among them hardly ever suspected what isolation there lurked behind that apostolic facade, hung with slogans about harmony and divine brotherly love. This passage from his diary of 1900 sounds like a muffled cry of despair, giving away one of his secrets: 'Dull, miserable state the whole day. Towards the evening this mood passed into tenderness—a desire for fond-

[1] The italics in this passage, taken from the draft of a letter which Tolstoy intended to leave for his wife, are mine.

ness, for love; I longed as children do to press up to a loving, pitying human being, to weep with emotion and to be comforted. But whom could I come close to like this? I think of all the people I loved, and not one of them can offer me all the sympathy I need. If I could be little again and snuggle up to my mother as I imagine her to myself! Yes, yes, mother whom I called to when I could not speak; she—my highest image of pure love; not cold, divine love, but earthly, warm, motherly. It is that for which my battered, weary soul is longing.'

What is all the pomp of fame in the face of such loneliness from which nothing could save him, least of all his preaching of divine brotherly love! But if so, there must have been two or even more Tolstoys: one on the surface, 'for show, for people', and the other the essential Tolstoy. Some knowledge of the latter is indispensable for any one who wants to understand the work and the personality of that great but disturbing figure.

II

The Art of Tolstoy (1)

AN author of Tolstoy's stature should be judged from the standpoint of his international as well as national significance. The verdicts of these two need not coincide. Byron, for example, is a greater figure in European literature as a whole than in the literature of his own country. The reverse is the case with Pushkin. No author means more to his own national literature than does Pushkin to the literature of Russia. Yet his international status still remains behind even that of Turgenev. As for Tolstoy, fame came to him abundantly from his own country and from abroad. But whereas in Russia it was Tolstoy the artist who was recognized and appreciated long before Tolstoy the preacher, abroad the case seemed to be the other way round. Still, in the end both agreed that, with all its peculiarities, Tolstoy's art was supreme. Hence it is necessary to point out at least some of its principal features.

When, at the beginning of the 'fifties, Tolstoy began to write, Russian prose was more or less at the crossroads. In Pushkin, Lermontov, and Gogol the purely narrative prose had already reached a climax which could hardly be surpassed. It was the critic Belinsky who tried to direct it along a new path, and this inaugurated the 'natural school' in Russian literature. He demanded from literature simplicity, sincerity, truth to life and at the same time also service to life which, in the 'forties, meant a humanitarian trend or purpose.

Belinsky's slogan fell on fertile soil. The principal evil of

Russia in those days—serfdom—soon became the bugbear of the new prose, from Grigorovitch's early tales and Turgenev's *A Sportsman's Sketches* onwards. It was in a similar spirit that the young Dostoevsky took up the 'insulted and the injured'. But here the Russian authors were faced by the problem of how to express their 'purpose' in terms of art instead of sermonizing propaganda. It was not an easy problem, especially later on—during the utilitarian 'sixties. Yet it had to be coped with. Realizing that literature was not for mere 'amusement', the Russian authors felt their moral and social responsibilities as authors—responsibilities which they endeavoured to reconcile with their aesthetic or artistic conscience. The most successful harmony between the two was achieved by Turgenev. But Turgenev was an essentially balanced genius who, being primarily an artist, never attempted to probe those depths of human life which were beyond his ken. Dostoevsky solved the problem by creating a new type of philosophic-psychological novel and that dynamic inner dialogue which he introduced into modern fiction as a whole. He, too, knew how to express his 'purpose', his 'idea' (or whatever you call it), in terms of art—at times most ingeniously so. Tolstoy, on the other hand, often fell precisely here between the two stools. It is all the more to his credit that, in spite of this, he yet remained a first-rate artist.

II

While reading Tolstoy's earlier works, one is repeatedly struck by what might be called his struggle for adequate self-expression. This may, perhaps, be the reason why so many of them remained unfinished. His trilogy, *Childhood-Boyhood-Youth,* represents the first three portions of a planned longer work (partly suggested by Rousseau's *Confessions* and modelled on Sterne's *Sentimental Journey*) which he never completed. His *A Landowner's Morning,* too, is only the opening part of a planned but never written *Novel of a Russian Landowner*. Nor did he finish his Caucasian narrative, *The Cossacks*. His other sketches from the Caucasus, such as *A Raid* and *Wood-Felling*, read either as episodes taken from some bigger narratives, or else as intensified pages from his own diary.

Even in these early works Tolstoy's predilection for character and situation, to the neglect of a rounded-up plot, is noticeable. Another feature is their transposed or indirect autobiographic character. Most of them might have been worked out from the pages of his diaries. Which brings us to the fact that, with an interval of fifteen years, Tolstoy actually wrote diaries from the age of eighteen to the end of his life. Minute observation, self-analysis, self-criticism, a strong didactic and moralizing propensity—such are the main characteristics of those diaries. Such are also at least some characteristics of his writings whose affinity with his diaries is beyond doubt. Tolstoy's very first attempt at authorship, *The History of Yesterday*,[1] dating from March 1851 (i.e. before he had written *Childhood*) can even be regarded as an amplified extract from a diary. From an artistic standpoint it is moreover typical of Tolstoy by its 'detailed thinking', its psychological imponderables, and its long sentences the only aim of which is to render everything as exact and concrete as possible.

Tolstoy the realist thus emerged already here, and he remained one to the end. He never 'invented' through the exercise of his fancy. He never indulged in complicated plots, but took everything straight from life as it passed through his own inner and external experience. Almost devoid of a purely inventive imagination, he was endowed with an incredible intuition for life which was the backbone of his art. So much so that his realism often became not only more significant, but also more real than reality itself. In his *Childhood*, for example, there is no plot, but only flashes of

[1] This work was printed for the first time only a few years ago.

a child's development up to his boyhood. Instead of a 'story' we have life itself, represented by some of its casual yet typical fragments under such unexciting titles as *Mamma, Papa, Lessons, Preparations for the Hunt, Games,* etc. In spite of this, one reads them with absorbing interest, since they afford us such unexpected and refreshing glimpses into a child's soul. What is more, Tolstoy knows how to conjure up the elusive poetic atmosphere of childhood without any deliberate poetic devices, so frequent in Turgenev's mellow prose.

It would hardly be possible to find a greater matter-of-fact realist than Tolstoy. Like Stendhal (from whom he learned quite a lot), he is at his best when dealing with things which can be visualized, analysed, and concretely experienced. The sober truth of life meant to him so much that he suspected at once anything that was not simple and natural enough in its expression. This was one reason why he disliked poetry and why he turned, later on, so savagely even against Shakespeare himself. From the very outset he cultivated the ordinary colloquial language of his class and indeed spared no pains to render his characters and surroundings as minutely and conscientiously as possible. What this kind of realism could be like is proved by all his works from *Sebastopol* to *Anna Karenina.* As an illustration his description of Vronsky's racing horse Frou-Frou in the latter novel can be quoted:

'Frou-Frou was of medium size and by no means free from blemish. She was slenderly built. Her chest, though well arched, was narrow. Her hindquarters tapered rather too much, and her legs, especially her hind legs, were perceptibly bowed inwards. Neither fore nor hind legs were particularly muscular, but on the other hand she was extremely broad in the girth, now that she was lean from her strict training. Seen from the front, her canon bones were fine and sharp, but unusually wide sideways. She appeared all the more narrow in build because so deep in the breadth. But she possessed in the highest degree a characteristic which made one forget all her defects. This was her thoroughbred quality—the kind of blood that *tells,* as they say in English. The muscles, clearly marked beneath the network of sinews, stretched in the fine, mobile skin, which was smooth as satin, seemed hard as bone. Her lean head with the prominent, bright, sparkling eyes, broadened out to her muzzle with its wide crimson nostrils. Her whole appearance, more especially about the head, was spirited but gentle. She was one of those creatures who seem as if they would certainly speak if only the mechanism of their mouths allowed them to.'

It is with the same thoroughness that Tolstoy introduces to us his characters. He not only shows them through a number of situations, but also through their typical gestures, their *tics,* their manner of speech, their soliloquies, until they stand before us as alive and three-dimensional as though they were our most intimate acquaintances. With all this he combines a vitality which passes at times into exuberance—not of a romantic kind, but of an overflow of life itself. It is enough to remember the zest with which Tolstoy describes certain episodes of his childhood and boyhood, countless scenes (especially the battle scenes) in *War and Peace,* the skating, horse-racing, hunting, and mowing in *Anna Karenina,* in order to realize how wonderfully the truth of life can be intensified and completed by the truth of art. Far from being a refuge from life, his art became both an affirmation and examination of life. And it was due to the different nature of these two functions that he later stumbled over the problem of his own vocation as an author. But on the whole, most of his writings before his conversion in 1879 were an affirmation of life even in the teeth of all his questioning. The spontaneity of his own zest for life is shown in his earliest writings, in *The Cossacks,* for instance, but without any romantic or 'poetic' descriptions. Take Olenin's (the chief character) first impressions of the Caucasian mountains.

'In the rapid motion of the vehicle over the even road, the mountains seemed to be running along the horizon with the summits gleaming in the rising sun. At first the mountains only surprised Olenin, but later they gave him pleasure. And later, as he gazed longer at this chain of snow-capped mountains, which were not connected with other black mountains, but rose directly from the steppe, he began by degree to understand their full beauty and to "feel" the mountains. From that moment, everything he saw, everything he thought, everything he felt, assumed for him a new, severely majestic character, that of the mountains. All the Moscow reminiscences, his shame and remorse, all the trite dreams of the Caucasus, everything disappeared, and never returned again. "Now it has begun," a solemn voice said to him. And the road and the distant line of Terek, and the villages, and the people, all appeared to him no longer a trifling matter. He looked at the sky, and he thought of the mountains. He looked at himself, and at Vanyusha (his servant)—and again the mountains. There, two Cossacks rode by, and their muskets in cases evenly vibrated on their backs, and their horses intermingled their chestnut and grey legs—and the mountains. The sun rose, and glistened on the Terek beyond the reeds—and the mountains. From the Cossack village came a native cart, and women, beautiful young women, walked—and the mountains. "Abreks (a hostile tribe) race through the steppes, and I am travelling, and fear them not: I have a gun, and strength, and youth—and the mountains." '

This passage could have been taken straight from the diary of an excited but hardly romantic youth, making his first acquaintance with the Caucasian mountains. And *the mountains* is here used by Tolstoy as a recurring suggestive nucleus for feelings which otherwise would require much longer and perhaps rhetorical descriptions. Tolstoy kept within the boundaries of sober realism even in this novel the Caucasian background of which had been made use of, and in the most glowing terms, by the Russian romantics. Yet the same Tolstoy who had solved the conflict between the truth of art and the truth of life in favour of the latter, had to face another and more painful clash: the one between his affirmation of life on the one hand, and his understanding of life on the other.

III

The process of the struggle between the two can again best be studied on certain pages of his diaries. His powerful instincts and his brooding thought seemed to diverge at a certain point to the extent of turning against each other. One of the tasks of his art was (in so far as his personal needs were concerned) how to bring the two together and to reconcile them in the end. This is a further reason why so many of his works are but disguised fragments of an autobiography, and why his great narrative art is much too often mixed with moralizing, to begin with some of his earliest writings: *Luzern, Albert, A Landowner's Morning, The Cossacks, Family Happiness,* etc.

This feature, moreover, gives a clue not only to the *raison d'être,* but also to the general structure of a number of his works. Their starting-point can usually be reduced to some problem or idea, in most cases a moral problem. Tolstoy's *Novel of a Russian Landowner,* for example, of which only a small part (*A Landowner's Morning*) had been written, was to be based on the problem: how to achieve a maximum of happiness in rural existence. *Family Happiness* dealt with the problem of personal happiness through married life. *The Cossacks,* too, with all its surface spontaneity, was a problem novel. *War and Peace* is full of problems and ideas. So is *Anna Karenina.* The 'idea' is not only illustrated or proved by the story, but acts at the same time as a unifying knot for the entire narrative. The unity between Tolstoy the artist and Tolstoy the didactic moralist was often far from organic. Yet such as it was, it determined more than once the structure of his works.

In order to turn a moral or other idea into a structural principle, Tolstoy often made use of the method of contrasts. But instead of showing his antitheses dramatically, he handled the theme in such a way as to transfer the reader in turns from one contrast to the other, until the basic idea underneath was brought out—through comparison—as concretely as possible. Thus the structure of his early story, *Three Deaths,* is based on the idea of the horror of death. The theme is worked out by means of three episodes each of which could stand independently of the other two. A similar parallelism is to be found in Tolstoy's third Sebastopol story. Another in his *Two Hussars* where, in the same parallel manner, two generations—the fathers and the sons—are contrasted. Whereas each separate part of such a story is treated with great artistic skill, the parts themselves are connected by means of the 'idea' which, as a rule, is not of an aesthetic but of a moral and didactic order.

In *War and Peace* the same principle is maintained, but the structure is of a more complex kind. It represents, first of all, two parallel and to some extent clashing novels. One of them is a domestic novel written in that homely language of the Russian gentry class which Tolstoy used in such a masterly way. The other novel is of a military kind, full of theoretical comments and discussions—often written in the style of a conscientious chronicle. Also in *Anna Karenina* we see the parallelism of two contrasted novels. Anna and Vronsky are the chief characters of one, Kitty and Levin of the other. If stress is laid on marriage as such, we actually have here a parallelism between three kinds of marriage. Karenin and Anna represent one of them, Levin and Kitty the second, Oblonsky and Dolly the third. All of them are woven into a pattern, dictated primarily by the underlying moral 'idea'. But since both *War and Peace* and *Anna Karenina* represent the peak of Tolstoy's creative genius, a little more should be said about them even in so short a survey as this.

Tolstoy wrote *War and Peace* for about six years. Such a long period might itself have been responsible for some of its formal vagaries. The novel had actually been planned at first as an ordinary family novel of manners. Its title was to be *All is Well that Ends Well.* Nor was it meant to be an historical novel. History was to provide only the background for those aspects of family life which are essentially above history with all its political changes and catastrophes. In the process of writing, however, Tolstoy was more and more carried away by the theme of Napoleon-Alexander, and by the decisive clash between the two in 1812. The background itself gradually expanded to such an extent (and for the most part independently of the author's first intentions) that it formed a parallel narrative or a chronicle of its own, written in a style befitting the subject. The two novels were then combined into one mainly by the basic 'idea' or ideas. The entire work then received a new title which Tolstoy probably borrowed from Proudhon's *La guerre et la paix*—a book he knew well.

According to the usual standards, *War and Peace* ought to be called an historical novel. But, strangely enough, it became more than that for the very reason that Tolstoy, in spite of his enormous intuition for people and things, actually lacked the historical sense required for such a task. There is plenty of life, there is also plenty of history in the novel, but on more than one occasion the two seem to be on different planes. Tolstoy's own comments on the military and historical happenings of the period often encumber the narrative to the point of weariness and could easily be left out. Moreover, in the process of writing Tolstoy analysed away history itself and in the end refused to assign it due significance. The actual centre of gravity is not on the historical and military, but on the 'domestic' side of the novel. The agitated background of the Napoleonic wars from 1805 onwards was, however, a good pretext for giving a cross-section of Russian life as a whole: from the Court to the cottage. From the aristocratic circles in Petersburg and Moscow one is transferred to the battlefields of Austria and Russia, then to the country-mansions with their old-fashioned squires and ways of life. With the same skill we are shown the feats of the Russian army, the burning of Moscow in 1812, the pillaging French soldiers, the small provincial towns crowded with refugees—in fact, the entire Russia awakening and reacting to the threat of the invader. The reader's attention is even more engaged by the purely domestic life, unfolded in this 'family chronicle' with the Rostovs and the Bolkonskys, i.e. Tolstoy's own paternal and maternal grandparents, in the centre. The marriage between Nicholas Rostov and Marie Bolkonskaya (Tolstoy's father and mother), and not Napoleon's downfall, forms the actual denouement of the novel. But before we reach it, we see Nikolay and other young folk in the Rostov household develop and mature, through all sorts of experiences—intensified and deepened by Tolstoy's art.

There are scores of individual characters in the novel, yet each of them can be recognized the moment he reappears, by his peculiar features and habits, even by the inflection of his voice. They seem to have a concrete existence of their own outside the printed page, and an existence so full-blooded and convincing that we cannot help taking a personal interest in their destinies. Their variety, too, is wellnigh inexhaustible: from the debonair and somewhat irresponsible old Count Rostov and the pedantic eighteenth-century *philosophe* Prince Bolkonsky to the good-natured 'bear' Pierre Bezoukhov, the brooding Prince Andrey Bolkonsky, the reckless Dolokhov and the pushing careerist Boris Drubetskoy with his priceless care-worn mother—the very quintessence of a 'poor relation'. Then the masterly women portraits from the 'beautiful animal' Hélène Kuragin to the pious and timid old maid Marie Bolkonskaya, or to Natasha Rostova—one of the finest portraits of a girl developing into a woman in all literature. Nor should be omitted the figures of the army leaders and officers, to begin with Napoleon and Kutuzov. Even Nikolay Rostov (Tolstoy's father), a decent mediocrity in every respect, imprints himself upon our mind as a memorable character. And all of them are treated with Tolstoy's intuitive insight into human nature. The only two exceptions are Alexander I and Napoleon. If the tsar is idealized, Napoleon is caricatured, and with evident malice. One of Tolstoy's critics (Ivanov-Razumnik) goes as far as to call this novel a war between Napoleon and Tolstoy.

Tolstoy's relative weakness came out only in his propensity for reasoning. As though anxious to fill the gap between the domestic and the military side of *War and Peace* with plenty of ideas, he even put forward a peculiar philosophy of history[1] which played a considerable part in his later attitudes and theories. In a subsequent edition (1873) the tedious military and philosophic discussions were actually dropped. The numerous French passages in the conversation (a mixture of Russian and French was quite in the style of the epoch, at least in the higher strata) were given only in Russian. Both were later restored. But the novel itself is so mighty a creative achievement that it redeems its own flaws. It is the nearest approach to a national epic in prose. The more so because this is Tolstoy's only work in which his Rus-

[1] The Soviet critic, K. Eikhenbaum, in his illuminating book, *Tolstoy in the 'Sixties,* points out that while writing *War and Peace* Tolstoy was influenced by Professor Pogodin's (a Russian follower of Schelling) *Paradoxes of History* (1836), to some extent by Proudhon and Joseph de Maistre. On the military side his Quixotic friend, Prince S. S. Urusov, gave him a number of suggestions.

Another stimulating work about Tolstoy's great novel is *The Materials and the Style in Tolstoy's Novel 'War and Peace'* by V. B. Shklovsky (1928, in Russian).

sian consciousness and even his national pride are displayed. At the same time it represents the peak of the gentry-class literature at a time when the guardianship of Russian culture had already passed from that class into the hands of the intelligentsia. And finally, it is both an affirmation and an encyclopaedia of life not only in time, but also in its timeless aspects; not only in history, but also outside, or even against history. We see life in its eternal flow, one generation displacing the other—wars or no wars, politics or no politics. All the youngsters who create such a refreshing springlike atmosphere in the Rostovs household, in due course grow up, take their appointed stations in life, while the older generations die or retreat. Natasha's nursery, in the Epilogue, the all-importance of her baby and its swaddling clothes, marks as it were the apotheosis of the biological continuity of life so dear to Tolstoy during those days.

Life as its own justification! Such would be the first conclusion. Yet it would be a superficial one. Life of this kind was not enough for Tolstoy—not even when it displayed its wealth as prodigally and generously as in *War and Peace*. He accepted its variety, but reserved his misgivings. Unable to accept life without a meaning of life, he put his own doubts and queries into Pierre Bezoukhov and Prince Andrey, both of them important characters of the novel. But however anxious their spiritual quest, it does not yet disturb the general tenor of *War and Peace* to the extent of undermining Tolstoy's cult of life. This happened, however, in a much stronger degree in his next great novel, *Anna Karenina*.

IV

This work, too, is partly a 'family chronicle', and in a more personal sense than *War and Peace*. The chapters about Kitty and Levin contain the history of Tolstoy's own love and marriage. Tolstoy the artist is here on the same height as in *War and Peace*. Tolstoy the man, however, has changed since then. The affirmation of life for its own sake, which dominated *War and Peace* even in the teeth of Pierre's and Prince Andrey's quest, here gradually gives way to Levin's anxious self-examination, and to a growing inquiry into problems connected with the aim and the meaning of life itself.

The structure of the novel is based on the parallelism of a double contrast. One of them is the 'Rousseauesque' contrast between the artificial and demoralizing complexities of city life as compared with the rooted existence in the countryside. By the countryside Tolstoy understood above all his own ancestral manor. For at that time he was still an inveterate landowner with rather conservative ideas and leanings. The second contrast, following from the first, is, however, one between the two principal couples: Kitty—Levin and Anna—Vronsky. While the more or less virtuous squire Levin and his immaculately virtuous Kitty settle down to a happy patriarchal existence, the beautiful adulteress Anna and her lover Vronsky find in their liaison no contentment and are crushed in the end by an inevitable catastrophe. Put in these terms, the theme may look much too bald. Yet what a wealth and depth of life was woven into such a seemingly commonplace motive—a wealth and depth of life which only Tolstoy was able to summon. 'I consider this novel so perfect of its kind that in poetic depth it can find no equal in any European literature of the nineteenth century. In some respects it stands even higher than *War and Peace*.' Such was the verdict of Constantine Leontyev, one of Tolstoy's shrewdest critics.

The background of the novel is partly Petersburg and Moscow with their aristocratic and higher bureaucratic circles, and partly Levin's country estate with the neighbouring districts. As in *War and Peace,* the stress is again on situations and characters, especially on characters, all of whom testify to Tolstoy's plastic genius at its best. How could one possibly forget Anna with her elusive yet overpowering beauty? Her husband—the correct bureaucrat Karenin, with his sticking-out ears and cracking finger-joints? The incurable *viveur* and charmer Stiva Oblonsky? Or Levin himself with all his caprices and worries, complicated (later on) by his inner torments? Here, as in *War and Peace,* even the most episodic character is alive to his finger-tips. And as in *War and Peace,* our attention is continually shifting like a kaleidoscope, from one sphere to the other: from Moscow to Petersburg, then to Levin's estate, to Kitty's stay in Germany, to Anna's stay in Italy, then to Russia once more. Tolstoy takes us through all social strata, with his unflagging artistic power and with his former zest for life. The latter comes out most spontaneously in him when he is nearest to earth. One feels it even in Levin's despondence, caused by his break with Kitty during the last period of his bachelor existence, as we can see from this episode referring to field work on his estate.

'The cart was tied up. Vanka (a village lad) jumped down and led the good-natured, well-fed horse by the bridle. The woman threw her rake on the cart and with a brisk gait, waving her arms about, she joined the other women who had assembled for the singing. Vanka reached the road and joined a long procession of carts. The women, with rakes over their shoulders, sparkling in their colours, followed the carts, singing in their merry, ringing voices. One wild, coarse voice started a song and sang it as far as the refrain, while fifty other voices, young, fresh, and powerful, took it up from the beginning and continued to the end. They drew near to Levin, swelling like a cloud of tumultuous joy. It seemed to envelop him and the haycock he was sitting on, the loaded carts, the whole field and the fields in the distance. Everything blended together and trembled with the measure of this wild, mirthful song and the shouting and whistling and clapping. Levin grew envious of this lusty mirth; he too would have liked to take part in the expression of this joy of life, yet he could do nothing but lie there and listen. When they were lost from view, and he could no longer hear their lively song, all the consciousness of his loneliness came upon him. He grew depressed at the sense of his own indolence and his inutility to the world at large.'

The reader's attention is divided principally between Levin and Anna, until the looming tragedy of Anna absorbs most of his interest. Anna is a tragic figure in the sense that it is precisely some of her finest qualities that bring about her ruin. Had she been just another Betsy, the tragedy would not even have touched her. In some respects she is the reverse of Tatyana in Pushkin's *Evgeny Onegin*.[1] Suffering as it were from a father fixation, she (like Tatyana) married the aged dignitary Karenin—more a father than a husband. When she had fallen in love with Vronsky, she (unlike Tatyana) followed the voice of her heart. She gave herself to Vronsky openly and honestly, and lived with him. But this betrayal of her father-substitute caused such ravages in her unconscious that, in spite of all her love for Vronsky, she was inwardly impelled to look for adequate punishment or self-punishment. Her suicide was only the final consummation of this process.

As is known, Tolstoy interprets her tragedy in terms of a moral retribution: not so much in its Christian sense as in the spirit of the Eastern Karma, and of depressing moral fatalism. This 'idea' does not impair, however, the skill with which he depicted all the phases of Anna's life as converging, and inevitably so, towards such an end; or his masterly analysis of the inner changes produced in her and in those concerned. The only flaw, and not a major one, is perhaps the insufficiently motivated suddenness of her falling in love with Vronsky. It has to be taken on credit, since Vronsky himself does not strike one either as big or interesting enough to

[1] Tolstoy based most of her physical features on Pushkin's beautiful daughter, Baroness Hartung.

evoke so strong a passion in such a woman as Anna. But a flaw of this kind hardly matters as compared with the excellence and fullness of the novel as a whole. Dostoevsky himself wrote about it in his *Journal of an Author* (1877): 'This is an unheard-of, a first-rate piece of work. Is there another author among us who could equal it? And who in Europe can offer us anything like it? Has there appeared in all their literatures, during the last few years, a single work which could be put beside this novel?'

The moral trend conspicuous in Tolstoy's treatment of Anna, found here a somewhat different channel of expression in Levin, or rather in Levin's vexation of spirit amid all his prosperity and happiness. As readers of the novel remember, his inner crisis became so acute as to bring him to the verge of suicide from which—significantly enough—he was saved by the wisdom of a primitive peasant. All the chapters dealing with Levin's inner quest and torments reflect the moral crisis of Tolstoy himself—a crisis which he afterwards described in his *Confession*.

III

The Art of Tolstoy (II)

ALTHOUGH most of Tolstoy's works, from his *Childhood* onwards, contained personal avowals in disguise, he drew up, at the age of fifty, a direct though condensed confession and launched it on the world. This account of his life, his inner crisis and the subsequent change that occurred in him is one of his most outstanding works. Written with that dynamic simplicity which is the reverse of rhetorics, it yet comprises passages imbued with a superb rhetorical inflection—one which enhances the author's frankness, instead of serving as a substitute for it. His *Confession* is thus remarkable both as a sustained literary achievement and as a personal document. It unveils before us a man grappling, entirely on his own, with the eternal problems of existence, of good and evil, of life and death. And Tolstoy's efforts to solve them were all the more pathetic because he wanted to conquer the truth with his bare hands, so to speak. Insufficiently equipped either with philosophic or scientific knowledge, he described for this very reason his own impasse as a drama latent in, and to be coped with, by every one of us.

'There is an Eastern fable,' he says, 'told long ago, of a traveller overtaken on a plain by an enraged beast. Escaping from the beast he gets into a dry well, but sees at the bottom of the well a dragon that has opened its jaws to swallow him. And the unfortunate man, not daring to climb out lest he should be destroyed by the enraged beast, and not daring to leap to the bottom of the well lest he should be eaten by the dragon, seizes a twig growing in a crack in the well and clings to it. His hands are growing weaker and he feels he will soon have to resign himself to the destruction that awaits him above or below, but still clings on. Then he sees that two mice, a black and a white one, go regularly round and round the stem of the twig to which he is clinging and gnaw at it. And soon the twig itself will snap and he will fall into the dragon's jaws. The traveller sees this and knows that he will inevitably perish; but while still hanging he looks around, sees some drops of honey on the leaves of the twig, reaches them with his tongue and licks them. So I too clung to the twig of life, knowing that the dragon of death was inevitably awaiting me, ready to tear me to pieces; and I could not understand why I had fallen into such torment. I tried to lick the honey which formerly consoled me, but the honey no longer gave me pleasure, and the white and black mice of day and night gnawed at the branch by which I hung. I saw the dragon clearly and the honey no longer tasted sweet. I only saw the inescapable dragon and the mice, and I could not tear my gaze from them. And this is not a fable but the real unanswerable truth intelligible to all.'

It was a conflict between life and the meaning of life in Tolstoy's own consciousness. He could accept no longer one without the other, yet his efforts to find a meaning led nowhere. 'I was like one lost in a wood, who, horrified at having lost his way, rushes about wishing to find the road. He knows that each step he takes confuses him more and more, but still he cannot help rushing about. It was indeed terrible. And to rid myself of the terror I wished to kill myself.' In short, it was Levin's impasse all over again. And, like Levin, Tolstoy instinctively turned for help not to the learned, but to the millions of simple people, tilling the land, and sustaining the life of us all. 'Indeed,' he asks, 'what are we who are convinced of the necessity of suicide, yet do not decide to commit it, but the weakest, most inconsistent, and, to put it plainly, the stupidest of men, fussing about with our own stupidity as a fool fusses about with a painted hussy? For our wisdom, however indubitable it may be, has not given us the meaning of life. But all mankind, who sustain life—millions of them—do not doubt the meaning of life. Indeed, from the most distant times of which I know anything, when life began, people have lived, knowing the argument about the vanity of life, which has shown me its senselessness, and yet they attributed some meaning to it.'

Tolstoy's *Confession* is thus an account of an up-to-date 'pilgrim's progress' of how he fought and erred on his path towards that meaning, and how its recovery affected his entire attitude towards life. It certainly stands as a milestone in both Tolstoy's life and work. For it was from that time on that the moral and didactic 'purpose' clung to Tolstoy's writings to the end. The ominous 'trunk', mentioned by Turgenev in 1880, became heavy indeed. In spite of that, it failed to undermine Tolstoy's artistic genius. The latter came out even in his deliberate campaign against art.

II

In his dogmatic and provocatively one-sided book, *What is Art,* Tolstoy demanded that art should transmit only morally valuable experiences, and in such a clear and simple language as to make them accessible to everybody. Art should above all 'infect'. And the excellence of a work of art is measured by the number of those 'infected' by it. The converted Tolstoy tried to live up to his theories not only by becoming deliberately didactic, but also by making himself understandable to as many readers as possible. For this reason he stripped his style and language to their bare essentials. In several works he made use of the highly idiomatic and laconic peasant language—a method clearly anticipated in his A B C book for children. In the 'eighties he even wrote a number of folk-stories (tales, parables, and legends based on traditional themes) in which he preserved the inimitable accent and flavour of the people's speech. However didactic these *Stories for the People* may be, the purpose, the contents, and the structure are so organically blended in them that we cannot separate one from the other. The same can be said of his morality play, *The First Distiller*. Although designed as an anti-alcoholic propaganda piece, it is a gem of its kind.

The artist and the moralist thus were not all the time at loggerheads even in Tolstoy's works after 1880. The periodic compromise—or, shall we say, armistice between the two—was actually responsible for some of Tolstoy's notable achievements. *The Death of Ivan Ilyitch,* for example, or *Master and Man* both of which are didactic and yet represent Tolstoy's art at its best. As usual, it is an 'idea'—a highly moral one—that serves as a compositional principle of either narrative. But at the same time the moral kernel is blended with the inner life of the characters concerned. With the exception of his last big novel, *Resurrection,* Tolstoy now gave up his former method of accumulating significant details and *petits faits.* He also paid less attention to the rounded up characters and was often anxious to point out what was typical of the whole group. Ivan Ilyitch is a kind of Everyman in the bureaucratic world. Brekhunov in *Master and Man* is something of a typical Russian *kulak* in general. Poznyshov in *The Kreutzer Sonata* is supposed to be a representative husband among the well-to-do people above a certain social line, etc. On the other hand, whenever Tolstoy reverted to the detailed method, he did so mainly in order to debunk and to indict. The inveterate anti-romantic in Tolstoy thus found full scope, however Utopian and fantastic some of his own tendencies may have become.

We should bear in our mind that even in his *Childhood* and *Boyhood* Tolstoy rebelled against the traditional sentimental-romantic attitude towards children by showing them exactly as they are. In *Sebastopol* he debunked the 'grandiose' romantic side of war and, incidentally, exposed (by delicate small touches) the eternal snobbery of man. In his Caucasian stories and sketches he undermined, moreover, that romantic side of the Caucasus which had been bequeathed to Tolstoy's generation by Pushkin and Lermontov and was still practised (on a 'popular' level) by the gushing storyteller Bestuzhev-Marlinsky. In spite of all its charm, *The Cossacks* can be regarded, in some respects, as a parody of the romantic tales of the Caucasus. Its hero, far from being a mysterious Byronic stranger, breaking the hearts of the native maidens, is himself contemptuously spurned by the Cossack girl Marianka who prefers a rowdy village lad to such a flower of Moscow society and culture as Olenin. Also in his posthumous *Hadji Murad* the 'romance' of the fighting with the Caucasian tribes is shown in all its stark and gruesome realism. As for his early works, it was in *Luzern* that he indicted modern civilized society. In *The Two Hussars* he did the same with regard to his own generation which he compared so unfavourably with that of the full-blooded fathers. In his first play, *A Poisoned Family* (written in the 'sixties but published only recently) Tolstoy ridiculed the young radicals of that period. His planned novel, *The Decembrists,* was to be an indictment of the 'sixties from the standpoint of an aged Decembrist returned from his exile in Siberia. Even in *War and Peace* he proceeded to debunk: official history, strategy, and hero-worship. After his conversion, however, he raised debunking itself to a moral duty which he exercised to the best of his abilities both as artist and pamphleteer. So much so that whenever he made use of his old saturated realism of details, he either mixed it with exhortations, or else turned it into a realism of indictment with the purpose of arousing our moral protest and disgust. The first aspect is illustrated by the very opening of his *Resurrection* which reads as follows.

'Though hundreds of thousands had done their very best to disfigure the small piece of land on which they were crowded together: paving the ground with stones, scraping away every vestige of vegetation, cutting down the trees, turning away birds and beasts, filling the air with the smoke of naphtha and coal—still spring was spring, even in the town. The sun shone warm, the air was balmy, the grass, where it did not get scraped away, revived and sprang up everywhere: between the paving-stones as well as on the narrow strips of lawn on the boulevards. The birches, the poplars, and the wild cherry-trees were unfolding their gummy and fragrant leaves, the bursting buds were swelling on the lime-trees; crows, sparrows, and pigeons, filled with the joy of spring, were getting their nests ready; the flies were buzzing along the walls warmed by the sunshine. All were glad: the plants, the insects, and the children. But men, grown-up men and women, did not leave off cheating and tormenting themselves and each other. It was not this spring morning men thought sacred and worthy of consideration, not the beauty of God's world, given for joy to all creatures—this beauty which inclines the heart to peace, to harmony, and to love—but only their own devices for enslaving one another.

'Thus, in the prison office of the Government town, it was not the fact that men and animals had received the grace and gladness of the spring that was considered sacred and important, but that a notice, numbered and with a superscription, had come the day before, ordering that on this, the 28th day of April, at 9 a.m., three prisoners now detained in the prison, a man and two women (one of these women, as the chief criminal, to be conducted separately), had to appear at the Court. So now, on the 28th of April, at eight o'clock in the morning, the chief jailer entered the dark, stinking corridor of the women's part of the prison.'

The moral trend of the novel is thus indicated without preliminaries—at the risk of repelling certain readers by its solemn and even sentimental note. The vigour of the former

Tolstoy is, however, felt in his realistic passages. These are particularly good when accompanied by his ironic tone and inflection—as, for instance, in the Law Court scenes. On the other hand, nothing is likelier to evoke our moral disgust than some of Tolstoy's seemingly detached matter-of-fact pictures. This description of the daily routine in the house-of-ill-fame, where Katyusha Maslova earned her living, is an example.

'Heavy sleep until late in the afternoon followed the orgies of the night. Between three and four o'clock came the weary getting up from a dirty bed, soda water, coffee, listless pacing up and down the room in bedgowns and dressing jackets, lazy gazing out of the windows from behind the drawn curtains, indolent disputes with one another; then washing, perfuming and anointing the body and hair, trying on dresses, disputes about them with the mistress of the house, surveying one's self in looking-glasses, painting the face, the eyebrows; fat, sweet food; then dressing in gaudy silks, exposing much of the body, and coming down into the ornamental and brilliantly illuminated drawing-room; then the arrival of visitors, music, dancing, sexual connexions with old and young and middle-ages, with lads and decrepit old men, bachelors, married men, merchants, clerks, Armenians, Jews, Tartars; rich and poor, sick and healthy, tipsy and sober, rough and tender, military men and civilians, students and mere schoolboys—of all classes, ages, and characters. And shouts and jokes, and brawls and music, and tobacco and wine, and wine and tobacco, from evening until daylight, no relief till morning, and then heavy sleep; the same every day and all the week. Then at the end came the visit to the police-station, as instituted by the Government, where doctors—men in the service of the Government—sometimes seriously, sometimes with playful levity, examined these women, completely destroying the modesty given as a protection not only to human beings but also the animals, and gave them the written permission to continue in the sins they and their accomplices had been committing all the week. Then followed another week of the same kind: always the same every night, summer and winter, workdays and holidays.'

Since Tolstoy's aim was no longer to justify life, but only the meaning of life, he did this either by reasoning or else by illustrating through forcible facts what was wrong with the whole of our existence. He did both in a number of pamphlets. Still, the artistic creator in him could not be silenced and had to come to terms with the moralist whom he often met half-way. Tolstoy's innovations, whether referring to language or to structure, helped to reconcile the two, at least in the best works written after his conversion.

III

His tendency to simplify the language has already been mentioned. But after 1880 even his favourite method of parallelism was reduced, on the whole, to contrasting in one and the same person two utterly different phases of life: separated by a sudden shock, or by some new truth in the light of which all his previous doings lost their importance and value. Tolstoy's own conversion as the central event of his life thus left its mark upon his literary creations of that period. His autobiographic but unfinished *Memoirs of a Madman* affords us a glimpse into the psychological state preceding such a crisis. The 'transvaluation of values' by which it was followed is, however, best shown in *The Death of Ivan Ilyitch.* Ivan Ilyitch's attitude towards life before and then during his illness (when he realized that death was imminent) are the two greatest possible contrasts. The same applies to Brekhunov's change in the face of death in the middle of a snow-covered plain. A conversion took place also in Poznyshov after his family drama. In *Father Sergius* we even see two conversions—one from pride and the other from humility. Tolstoy's naturalistic peasant drama, *The Power of Darkness,* also ends with a confession and conversion. The unfinished autobiographic play, *The Light Shines in Darkness,* shows the difficulties of a converted man of his own circle in coping with the normal circumstances of life. The entire novel of *Resurrection* is based on Nekhlyudov's conversion, even if Nekhlyudov resembles a moral loudspeaker of Tolstoy himself rather than a character made of flesh and blood. The list could be extended.

It goes without saying that in such stories the inner change of the chief character becomes the organizing principle not only with regard to psychology, but also with regard to form. Everything has to be arranged in such a manner as to converge towards the transformation of the character and to stress the change itself as compared with his previous stage. The change is a moral one and goes hand-in-hand with a transvaluation in the name of the new truth perceived. Some of his conversion stories, such as *The Kreutzer Sonata,* or *Father Sergius,* also contain the motive of sexual obsession—a motive which Tolstoy worked out with great power in his posthumous story, *The Devil.* And since this story has a bearing upon Tolstoy himself, its contents can be summed up as follows. A young landowner who, on the completion of his studies, returns to his estate, does not live up to the moral command of sexual continence. He contracts a liaison with a married peasant woman whose lust stirs up his passion to the uttermost. Later he falls in love with an innocent girl of his own class, marries her, and starts a new life, determined to remain loyal and faithful to her. But something goes wrong with his marriage. During his wife's confinement he chances to see repeatedly his former mistress—as lusty and seductive as ever. At first he hardly pays any attention to her. Gradually, her animal nature gets hold not only of his memory and imagination, but also of his senses. He becomes like one possessed by the desire to have her again, and this in spite of his sincere love for his wife. When the dilemma reaches its climax he finds no other outlet than suicide. In another version of the denouement he kills the 'devil', i.e. his temptress.

It would be hard to find another author whose moral condemnation of sensual lust goes hand-in-hand with such 'infectious' descriptions of sensuality as in Tolstoy. Even in *Resurrection,* one of the most stirring scenes is young Nekhlyudov's seduction of the pretty and innocent chambermaid Katyusha. There is something beyond mere pathology in the scene when the austere Father Sergius falls a prey to a lusty imbecile girl. And is it possible to convey a more condensed state of sexual obsession than Tolstoy does in *The Devil*? Did Tolstoy tease and stir up his own latent sensuality to a pitch in order to defy it, to put a moral 'chain' on it, at the most dangerous moment? Or was he impelled to gaze at it, now and then, because he could not help it? There is a border-line where excessive morality comes very close to its own opposite, as it were.

But the problem of a moral life is not only a private matter. It depends also on our social and political system, on the pattern of our civilization. If this happens to be at fault, the whole of human existence will have a wrong direction. It was above all Tolstoy's moral zeal that made him examine the entire structure of our civilization and reject it not only as immoral but also inhuman. His sympathy with the primitives had been strong enough even before. The peasant Karatayev in *War and Peace* is a proof. After his conversion, however, his affection for the peasant masses grew in the same ratio as did his negative attitude towards our civilization in general. And whenever a comparison between the social tops and the bottoms was possible, the former got the worst of it.

Tolstoy's sympathy with the masses was fostered, amongst other things, by his disgust with everything which his own class stood for. And since the latter represented the civilized ways of life, Tolstoy did his best to debunk those ways—to show their vulgarity, emptiness, and lack of purpose. *The Kreutzer Sonata* was an attack on their marriage. *The Death of Ivan Ilyitch* was an onslaught upon their 'accepted' routine of existence. In *Resurrection,* however, all the aspects and institutions, the Church and the State included, are pulled to bits with a merciless realism, at times even with merciless irony. Realism and irony now collaborated in Tolstoy's works with a stronger effect than ever before. It is not so much direct irony as irony between the lines. Sometimes an entire situation is shown in such a perspective that even the most obvious words and gestures of the characters concerned cannot help becoming irony in action. Tolstoy reached perfection of this kind in the often quoted scene between Ivan Ilyitch's mourning wife and her husband's two colleagues (Pyotr Ivanovitch and Schwarts) who came to pay the last respects to Ivan Ilyitch lying on the bier.

'Pyotr Ivanovitch once more crossed himself hurriedly, and, as it struck him, too hurriedly, not quite in accordance with the proprieties, turned and went to the door. Schwarts was waiting for him in the adjoining room, standing with his legs apart and both hands behind his back playing with his top hat. A single glance at the playful, sleek, and elegant figure of Schwarts revived Pyotr Ivanovitch. He felt that he, Schwarts, was above it, and would not give way to depressing impressions. The mere sight of him said plainly: the incident of the service over the body of Ivan Ilyitch cannot possibly constitute a sufficient ground for recognizing the business of the session suspended,—in other words, in no way can it hinder us from shuffling and cutting a pack of cards this evening, while the footman sets four unsanctified candles on the table for us; in fact, there is no ground for supposing that this incident could prevent us from spending the evening agreeably. He said as much indeed to Pyotr Ivanovitch as he came out, proposing that the party should meet at Fyodor Vassilyevitch's. But apparently it was Pyotr Ivanovitch's destiny not to play "screw" that evening. Praskovya Fyodorovna, a short, fat woman who, in spite of all efforts in a contrary direction, was steadily growing broader from her shoulders downwards, all in black, with lace on her head and her eyebrows as queerly arched as the lady standing beside the coffin, came out of her own apartments with some other ladies, and conducting them to the dead man's room, said: "The service will take place immediately; come in."

'Schwarts, making an indefinite bow, stood still, obviously neither accepting nor declining this invitation. Praskovya Fyodorovna, recognizing Pyotr Ivanovitch, sighed, went right up to him, took his hand, and said, "I know that you were a true friend of Ivan Ilyitch's . . .", and looked at him, expecting from him the suitable action in response to these words. Pyotr Ivanovitch knew that just as before he had to cross himself, now what he had to do was to press her hand, to sigh and to say, "Ah, I was indeed!" And he did so. And as he did so, he felt that the desired result had been attained; that he was touched and she was touched.

' "Come, since it's not begun yet, I have something I want to say to you," said the widow. "Give me your arm."

'Pyotr Ivanovitch gave her his arm, and they moved towards the inner rooms, passing Schwarts, who winked gloomily at Pyotr Ivanovitch.

' "So much for our 'screw'! Don't complain if we find another partner. You can make a fifth when you do get away," said his humorous glance.

'Pyotr Ivanovitch sighed still more deeply and despondently, and Praskovya Fyodorovna pressed his hand gratefully. Going into her drawing-room, that was upholstered with pink cretonne and lighted by a dismal-looking lamp, they sat down at the table, she on a sofa and Pyotr Ivanovitch on a low ottoman with deranged springs which yielded spasmodically under his weight. Praskovya Fyodorovna was going to warn him to sit on another seat, but felt such a recommendation out of keeping with her position, and changed her mind. . . .

' "I see to everything myself," she said to Pyotr Ivanovitch, moving on one side the albums that lay on the table; and noticing that the table was in danger from the cigarette ash, she promptly passed an ash-tray to Pyotr Ivanovitch, and said: "I consider it affectation to pretend that my grief prevents me from looking after practical matters. On the contrary, if anything could—not console me . . . but distract me, it is seeing after everything for him." She took out her handkerchief, as though preparing to weep again; and suddenly, as though struggling with herself, she shook herself, and began speaking calmly: "But I've business to talk about with you."

'Pyotr Ivanovitch bowed, carefully keeping in check the springs of the ottoman, which had at once begun quivering under him.

' "The last few days his sufferings were awful."

' "Did he suffer very much?" asked Pyotr Ivanovitch.

' "Oh, awfully! For the last moments, hours indeed, he never left off screaming. For three days and nights in succession he screamed incessantly. It was insufferable. I can't understand how I bore it; one could hear it through three closed doors. Ah, what I suffered!"

'After various observations about the details of the truly awful physical sufferings endured by Ivan Ilyitch (these details Pyotr Ivanovitch learned only through the effect Ivan Ilyitch's agonies had had on the nerves of Praskovya Fyodorovna), the widow apparently thought it time to get to business.

' "Ah, Pyotr Ivanovitch, how hard it is, how awfully, awfully hard!" and she began to cry again.

'Pyotr Ivanovitch sighed, and waited for her to blow her

nose. When she had done so, he said, "Indeed it is," and again she began to talk, and brought out what was evidently the business she wished to discuss with him; that business consisted in the inquiry as to how on the occasion of her husband's death she was to obtain a grant from the government. She made a show of asking Pyotr Ivanovitch's advice about a pension. But he perceived that she knew already to the minutest details, what he did not know himself, indeed, everything that could be got out of the government on the ground of this death; but that what she wanted to find out was, whether there were not any means of obtaining a little more? Pyotr Ivanovitch tried to imagine such means; but after pondering a little, and out of politeness abusing the government for its stinginess, he said that he believed that it was impossible to obtain more. Then she sighed and began unmistakably looking about for an excuse for getting rid of her visitor. He perceived this, put out his cigarette, got up, pressed her hand, and went out into the passage.'

IV

We quoted this scene in full, because its apparent matter-of-factness only increases the author's irony. The debunking of the obligatory *comme il faut* hypocrisy could hardly be done with more discreet and at the same time cruel touches. On the other hand, *The Death of Ivan Ilyitch* is one of those stories in which art and 'purpose' actually coincide and help each other, in spite of the growing gap between the ethical and the aesthetic values in Tolstoy's consciousness.

'The aesthetical and the ethical are only the two arms of one and the same lever; to the same extent as you lengthen and lighten one side, you shorten and make heavier the other. Once a man has lost his moral sense, he becomes particularly responsive to aesthetic sensations.' Thus wrote Tolstoy in his diary in August 1897. The whole of his *What is Art,* dating from the same period, is indeed nothing but an apology for such an attitude. Which does not mean that he kept to it to the letter. Purpose or no purpose, Tolstoy could not help being an artist, once he set out to tell a story. Yet he declared a fierce and dogmatic war on art at the very moment when nothing seemed to be beyond the range of his own artistic power. And the ruthlessness with which he turned even against his own former creations can only be explained by the fact that, for some reason or other, his attacks were disguised attacks directed primarily against himself. While reading him, it is not difficult to notice that, time and again, he was impelled to attack himself as though warding off certain dangers besetting his inner life. And when these became particularly strong, his countermeasures, too, had to become adequate. So Tolstoy's works are largely a record of his own inner conflict or conflicts the nature of which may perhaps afford us a few glimpses into his strange and complicated personality.

IV

Tolstoy's Dilemma

TOLSTOY himself encouraged the view that his life and writings were divided into two different parts, sharply separated by his conversion. A careful study of his entire work, letters and diaries included, makes one, however, unable to agree with this. There was neither an unexpected nor even a definite rupture between the two phases of Tolstoy's life. What happened was only a change of proportion between them, or rather a kind of shifting of the centre of gravity from one on to the other—a process which, far from eliminating Tolstoy's inner conflict, actually increased it. This conflict was all the more difficult, because in him it was a part of the psychological make-up which can be traced back to his earliest years.

Already in *Childhood, Boyhood, Youth,* Tolstoy gave quite a few clues to the discord of his nature, which consisted above all in the parallel working of his instincts and emotions on the one hand, and of his cold, detached observation and self-analysis on the other. Thus while describing the genuine grief he felt at his first departure from home, he remarks with his usual frankness: 'I was choking with tears, and something oppressed my throat so that I was afraid I would stifle. As we entered the highway, we saw a white handkerchief which some one was waving from the balcony. I began to wave mine, and this movement calmed me somewhat. I continued to cry, and the thought that my tears proved my sensitiveness afforded me pleasure and consolation.' The last sentence is revealing. However sincere his emotions, he could not help registering, even at that tender age, his mental and moral reactions which were equally prone to be accompanied by self-gratification or else self-reproach, as we can see from the following description of his first great sorrow. 'Before and after the burial, I never ceased to weep, and was sad; but it puts me to shame to recall that sadness, because a feeling of self-love was mingled with it; at one time the desire to show that I was more sorry than anybody else; again solicitude as to the impression which I was producing upon others; at another time, an aimless curiosity which caused me to make observations upon Mimi's cap and the faces of those present. I despised myself because the feeling I experienced was not exclusively one of sorrow, and I tried to conceal all others; for this reason my regret was insincere and unnatural. Moreover, I experienced a sort of pleasure in knowing that I was unhappy. I tried to arouse my consciousness of unhappiness, and this egotistical feeling, more than all the rest, stifled genuine grief within me.'

No matter how deep and spontaneous his emotions, the cold blade of analysis was there, too, ready to observe, to dissect, and very often also to condemn. The obvious result of such a habit is a growing awareness of one's own failings, of what is 'not right'. But the same awareness can be applied to others—as a safety measure against the feeling of one's own moral inferiority. One's faults are much easier to bear when one finds them in other people, too. And if the others camouflage them by means of respectable and virtuous appearances, then the appearances themselves must be shown up. A merciless criticism of what is behind them may also give one the illusion that one is at least potentially better than those whom one criticizes and unmasks. On this condition one is even ready to indulge in self-reproaches, repentance, and resolutions to improve. The more so because they all serve as a proof of one's latent goodness or even potential moral superiority. A disposition of this kind can actually land one in moral dangers from the other end: one is so easily tempted to commit reprehensible actions, not because one likes them, but because one enjoys the luxury of remorse and of virtuous resolutions after them. The spiritual pleasure, obtained from repentance and from the plans for moral regeneration and self-perfection can even be increased by a sinful past. Or, if it is not sinful enough, one makes it so by depicting it as much blacker than it really is.

'The principal feeling was disgust at myself and remorse,' Tolstoy confesses in his *Youth,* 'but a remorse so mingled with hope of bliss that there was nothing sorrowful about it. It seemed to me so easy and so natural to tear myself from all the past, to reconstruct, to forget everything which had been, and to begin my life with all its relations quite anew, that the past neither weighed nor fettered me. I even took pleasure in my repugnance to the past, and began to see it in more sombre colours than it possessed. The blacker was the circle of memories of the past, the purer and brighter did the pure, bright point of the present and the rainbow hues of the future stand out in relief against it. The voice of remorse, and the passionate desire to perfection, was the chief new spiritual sentiment of that epoch in my spiritual development.'

The last sentence is an understatement. The 'voice of remorse and the passionate desire to perfection' remained one of Tolstoy's dominant features, as well as a moral stimulus, throughout the whole of his life. But a person in whom the will to reform plays such an important part is naturally on the look-out for rules and principles in the name of which he could attain the height of perfection. The more he is afraid of his own 'dark' impulses and passions, the more unconditionally will he cling to those rules—until the next fall. Nor will he stop there. The rules adopted by him must have a universal validity if they are to be valid at all, and his duty is to endorse them for the benefit of the world. What is good for his personal salvation, must be good for the salvation of all.

It is at this point that moral perfection and latent moral pride often meet. They can even coincide—especially in the case of shy natures who want to overcome their feeling of inferiority by some great task which would exalt them not only in their own eyes but also in the eyes of other people, of the whole of mankind. To quote from Tolstoy's *Boyhood*: 'I often fancied myself a great man, who was discovering new truths for the benefit of mankind, and I gazed upon other mortals with a proud consciousness of my worth; but strange to say, when I came in contact with these mortals, I was shy in the presence of every one of them, and the higher I rated myself in my own opinion, the less capable I was of displaying my consciousness of my own merits to others, and could not even accustom myself not to feel ashamed of my every word and movement, however simple.'

Even Tolstoy's provocative self-assertiveness, after his first literary successes, was only a manœuvre with which to counter his own weakness and shyness. At the same time he kept on watching and analysing himself, as though he were dissecting a stranger in whose mental and moral reactions he was intensely interested. The diary thus became a habit, a need with him. What this need amounted to in the end is best shown by the fact that even during the most fateful hours of his life—while fleeing from his family and home—Tolstoy could not help observing and even *writing down* the minutest details of his flight. 'I trembled at the thought that she (his wife) would hear and come out. There would have been scenes, hysteria, and afterwards no getting away without an upset. At six o'clock everything was packed somehow and I went to the stable to tell them to harness. It was still night—pitch dark. I missed the path to the wing of the house, stumbled into a thicket, pricking myself, ran into the trees, fell, lost my cap and could not find it, made my way out with difficulty and went back to the house,' etc., etc.

II

The ability to observe one's actions in such detail at such a moment presupposes self-consciousness and detachment, both of which were unusually strong in Tolstoy. But so was the spontaneity of his instincts through which he sensed and experienced the fundamentals of life more deeply, more fully than can be said of ordinary mortals. His surplus of vitality (in the biological and 'pagan' meaning of the word) was so great that a cold moral censorship actually became necessary to him as a disciplinary measure. At the same time, there seemed to be no working balance or even contact between the two: each of them functioned on its own. On the one hand, there was the irrational *élan* of his instincts and passions, and on the other—the frowning and reasoning moralist, always ready to step in, to interfere and to disprove. The tension between such incompatible elements was responsible for a number of contradictions in Tolstoy's personality and work. On the whole, up to his conversion it was the spontaneous Tolstoy with his love of life who prevailed even in the teeth of his moralizing double; while after his conversion the moralist in him became menacing enough to make him turn against life—in the name of an abstract and highly moral meaning of life. But even apart from such a sharp division, he was tossed between the two directions from his youth until his last years, unable either to reconcile them or else to suppress one on behalf of the other.

This duality of his inner make-up is reflected even in his early works. One of the memorable chapters in *The Cossacks,* the description of Olenin's hunt in the Caucasian forest, provides a good illustration. When Olenin (i.e. the young Tolstoy himself) discovered a stag's lair in the thicket, he experienced the ecstasy of a true hunting savage. Each trifle around—the foliage, the imprints of the stag's knees, even the stag's dung—increased his joy, his pagan oneness with all nature. All at once he 'was overcome by such a strange feeling of causeless happiness and love for everything that, following an old boyish habit, he began to cross himself and to thank somebody for something. It suddenly passed through his mind with extraordinary clearness that he, Dmitry Olenin, a being apart from all other beings, was sitting all alone, God knew where, in the very spot where there used to live a stag, a beautiful old stag which, perhaps, had never before seen a man, and in a place where, perhaps, no one had been sitting before, or thinking about the same matter. "I am sitting here, and all about me are young and old trees, and one of these is festooned with wild grape vines; near me pheasants are fluttering, driving each other from their hiding-places, and probably scenting their dead brothers." He put his fingers on his pheasants, examined them, and wiped his hand, which was stained by their warm blood, against his mantle. "The jackals are probably scenting them, and with dissatisfied faces turning away in the opposite direction. The gnats fly all around me, passing by leaves that appear to them like many huge islands, and they hover in the air and buzz: one, two, three, four, one hundred, one thousand, a million gnats, and all of them buzz something, for some reason, all about me, and every one of them is just such a Dmitry Olenin, apart from all the rest as I am." He had a clear idea of what the gnats were thinking and buzzing. "Here, boys! Here is one whom we can eat," they buzzed and clung to him. And it became clear to him that he was not at all a Russian nobleman, a member of Moscow society, a friend and relative of this or that person, but simply just such a gnat, or pheasant, or stag, as those that now were living all around him. "I shall live and die, just like them, like Uncle Eroshka." And he is telling the truth: "Only grass will grow up!"

'"And what of it if the grass will grow up," he continued his thought. "Still I must live; I must be happy because I wish for this—happiness. It matters not what I am: such an animal as the rest, over which the grass will grow, and nothing else, or a frame into which a part of the One God has been encased,—I must still live the best way possible. But how must I live in order to be happy, and why have I not been happy before?" And he began to recall his former life, and he was disgusted with himself. He represented himself as an exacting egoist, whereas is reality he needed very little for himself. And he kept gazing about him: at the foliage checkered by the sunlight, at the declining sun, at the clear heaven, and he felt as happy as before. "Why am I happy, and why have I lived before?" he thought. "How exacting I used to be! How I concocted and caused nothing but shame and woe for myself!" And suddenly it seemed that a new world was open to him. "Happiness is this," he said to himself: "happiness consists in living for others. This is clear. The desire for happiness is inborn in man; consequently it is legitimate. In attempting to satisfy it in an egoistical manner, that is, by seeking wealth, glory, comforts of life, and love, the circumstances may so arrange themselves that it is impossible to satisfy these desires. Consequently these desires are illegitimate, but the need of happiness is not illegitimate. Now, what desires are these that can always be satisfied, in spite of external conditions? What desires? Love, self-sacrifice!" He was so rejoiced and excited when he discovered this truth which seemed to be new, that he leaped up and impatiently began to look around for some one to sacrifice himself for, to do good to and to love. "I do not need anything for myself," he proceeded in his thought, "then why should I not live for others?"'

So in the very midst of his pantheistic intimacy with Nature, Olenin began to recall his former life and felt disgusted with himself. He identified himself so intensely with the life around, the biting gnats included, that the overflow of his emotion can only be defined as the bliss of oneness. Yet even here the voice of his reasoning and moralizing double intruded—largely in order to weigh the selfish personal advantages of his selfless love. In the end, Olenin accepted such love because he found it less painful and therefore more profitable than selfishness. Without even noticing the naïve utilitarianism of his conclusion, he was so impatient of its results that he immediately wanted to put the newly discovered 'rule' into practice.

The utilitarianism of some of Tolstoy's other heroes too (with whom he is in sympathy) would be gross if it were not so naïve and primitive. The most blatant example is Nicholas Rostov (in *War and Peace*) in whom there is not even a pretence of Olenin's 'selflessness'. Having betrayed his sweetheart Sonya in order to marry an heiress, Rostov was not only prosperous but even happy ever after. And this is Tolstoy's own comment: 'Doubtless because Nicholas did not allow himself to entertain the idea that he was doing anything for the sake of others, or for the sake of virtue, everything he did was fruitful. His fortune rapidly increased; the neighbouring serfs came to beg him to purchase them, and long after his death the peasants preserved a memory of his rule.' In *Anna Karenina* again the squire Levin frankly confesses to his half-brother Koznyshov his own indifference to the peasants' welfare and education. He puts the final touch to it by the remark that 'no activity can be sound unless it is founded on personal interest'. Let us not forget that Levin is Tolstoy's own portrait during his prosperous 'squire period', after his marriage.

Yet when the moralist began to speak, the same Tolstoy turned against all personal interests with unexampled vehemence. Nor was this the only contradiction of which he was guilty. It is well known that in his young days Tolstoy was far from neglecting the dissipations of the *jeunesse dorée*.

Here, too, as in so many other experiences, he never stopped half-way. And as usual, after each bout he suffered from a moral aftermath, full of self-reproaches and resolutions which formed the greatest contrast to his actual life. 'Two principal passions which I have noted in myself are a passion for play and vanity; which latter is the more dangerous in that it assumes a countless multitude of different forms, such as a desire to show off, want of reflection and absence of mind, and so on', he wrote in 1851, while at Yasnaya Polyana. After pages of self-accusations on account of his sloth, weakness, lying, voluptuousness, and quite an impressive catalogue of other defects, he adds: 'Yesterday could not forbear signalling to some one in a pink dress who looked comely from a distance. Opened the back door, and she entered. Could not even see her; all seemed foul and repellent, and I actually hated her.'

Sensual by nature, Tolstoy was endowed with exceptionally strong passions. These he could keep in check only by exceptionally severe 'rules', according to which he endeavoured to map out his existence beforehand, from his student years onwards. His diaries of that period are interspersed with them. 'Also the fact that I find it necessary to determine my occupation beforehand renders a diary additionally indispensable,' he argued with himself in 1851. 'Indeed, I should like to acquire a habit of predetermining my form of life not merely for a day, but for a year, several years, the rest of my existence. This, however, will be too difficult for me, almost impossible. Nevertheless, I will make an attempt—at first for a day, then for two. In fact, as many days as I may remain loyal to my resolutions, for so many days will I plan beforehand.' There follow minute recipes for his moral conduct, behaviour in society, and even a few rules for playing at cards. 'Yesterday the day passed well enough,' he wrote on June 9th in the same year, 'for almost everything in it was carried out. With one point only I am feeling dissatisfied, and that point is the fact that I cannot overcome my sensuality, and the less so in that it is a passion which has now become a habit with me. However, my resolutions for two days having been carried out, I will make plans for a similar period.' But all came to nothing. On December 29th he again accused himself of leading the life of a brute. 'I have abandoned all my pursuits, and am feeling out of spirits. To-morrow I must rise early, and, until two o'clock, neither receive any one nor go out for a drive. . . . In the morning I will work at the table, read, and either play the piano or write something on music; while in the evening I will frame further rules and visit the tsiganes (gypsies).'

III

It is remarkable that the young Tolstoy could so easily combine his moral rules and resolutions with a visit to the gypsies: actually to the gypsy-girls who sang in fashionable restaurants and were perhaps willing to render also more intimate services when required. But the 'broader' and stronger the impulses of Tolstoy the man, the stricter had to be the rules of Tolstoy the moralist. Clear reasoned out formulae as to what was right and what was not right were the only weapon with which he hoped to curb the full-blooded irrational man within him, but the struggle was a long one and often futile.

The tension of this struggle is reflected in most of his works. In *War and Peace,* for example, there are scores of individual characters—all of them swayed on by that spontaneous stream of life which is beyond good and evil; which defies, as it were, all theories and philosophies of life. Yet neither Prince Andrey Bolkonsky nor Pierre Bezoukhov (Tolstoy's two doubles) could accept life without a philosophy, or rather without a meaning of life. This quest became later intensified in Levin (*Anna Karenina*) to such an extent that Tolstoy's personal *Confession,* written in 1879, and all that followed, was the only logical alternative to complete negation or even to suicide.

Needless to say that Tolstoy the artist is at his best when free from any interference on the part of his moral chaperon. His best pages are those in which he describes the breadth of life spontaneously: as he feels it pulsing and vibrating in his own blood, in his instincts. This is why he is so successful in rendering such characters as Uncle Eroshka with his wisdom of Nature in *The Cossacks*; the reckless Dolokhov in *War and Peace*; or the tough half-savage rebel Hadji Murad in the posthumous novel under the same title. Moreover, it is precisely this wisdom and law of intense life that often prompts to Tolstoy the artist such attitudes as have nothing in common with Tolstoy the seeker. Here is an example.

Olenin in *The Cossacks* first wants to sacrifice his own personal life for the benefit of others; but soon he himself admits that 'self-renunciation is nonsense, wild rambling. It is nothing but pride, a refuge from a well-deserved misfortune, a salvation from envying another's happiness. To live for others, to do good! Wherefore? When my soul is filled with the one love of myself, and with the one desire to love her [the Cossack girl Marianka] and live with her, to live her life. I now wish happiness, not for others, not for Lukashka [Marianka's sweetheart]. Now I do not love others. Formerly I should have said that this is bad. I should have tormented myself with the question, "What will become of her, of me, of Lukashka?" Now it is all the same to me. I suffer; but formerly I was dead, and now I live.' This is how life takes its own in the very teeth of moral rules and categories. Similarly, Sonya in *War and Peace* is condemned—with Tolstoy's approval—on account of her exaggerated goodness and selflessness. ' "To him that hath shall be given, and from him that hath not, shall be taken even that which he hath", do you remember?' says the prosperous and happy Natasha to her prosperous and happy husband Pierre. And this is her conclusion: 'She is that hath not; why, I don't know; perhaps she has no egoism. . . . She is a barren flower, you know, like what one finds among the strawberry flowers.'

Thus the first Tolstoy, who was more in love with life than with the rules (whether moral or otherwise) about life. And he himself was capable of showing, at least during his 'squire period', that crude biological assertion of life, which is not beyond but simply outside any moral categories. 'I am entirely uninterested in knowing as to who oppresses the Poles, or who has conquered Schleswig-Holstein. The butcher kills the ox we eat, and I cannot be compelled either to blame him, or to express my sympathy.' These lines, hardly redolent of a humanitarian moralist, are taken from one of Tolstoy's letters written soon after the tragic Polish debacle of 1863–4. The case could not be put more plainly, yet it is Tolstoy's primitive and amoral life-instinct rather than cynicism that comes out in those words. It is Uncle Eroshka all over again, although he probably would have put it into milder and more humane terms.

This does not mean that the other Tolstoy—Tolstoy the moralist and seeker—was insincere when preaching with even greater persistence views of the opposite kind. His sincerity was beyond doubt, but it was on a plane which ran parallel to the plane of his life-instincts, without as it were touching it. It was a conflict between two contradictory planes of sincerity in one and the same consciousness. Unable to integrate, or even to reconcile them, Tolstoy was actually compelled to put up with their simultaneity or, in the best case, with their alternation. The most puzzling and often painful feature about it was, however, the fact that no matter with which trend he sided, he could not feel entirely sincere in his allegiance, since his sincerity, too, was split up between opposite impulses and directions. It was partly this uncertainty, or vacillation, that made him so terribly frank, at times, about his own faults and defects. Exaggerated frankness served here as a proof, or at least an illusion, of complete sincerity. Yet the problem of sincerity is more complicated than that of frankness. It is easy to be perfectly frank even about one's insincerity. But how can one be truly sincere, as long as one is tossed—at one and the same time—between utterly conflicting emotions, ideas, and values, each of them insisting on its own rights? Rousseau's *Confessions*, for example, was incredibly frank. But in how far was it really sincere? What were its hidden conscious or unconscious motives? Exaggerated frankness may certainly be a proof of our will to complete sincerity. On the other hand, its very exaggerations can land us in untruthfulness from the other end. Who would ever believe Tolstoy literally when he accuses himself in his own *Confession*: 'Lying, robbery, adultery, drunkenness, violence, murder—there was no crime I did not commit'?

The situation becomes even worse when one suspects the same inability of being entirely sincere also in others. Or when one is so determined to prove that other human beings are even less sincere than oneself, that in the end one is haunted by their supposed hypocrisy. But for this very reason one takes a peculiar pleasure in unmasking and debunking their shams—a process which may assume enormous proportions when moral pathos is added to it.

According to the writer Vsevolod Garshin, Tolstoy (whom he knew personally) actually thought that all good men are mere hypocrites pretending to be good. Turgenev, whose generosity and fairness of judgment can hardly be questioned, was even more outspoken. 'Tolstoy had early developed', so he says, 'a feature which became the very basis of his gloomy world-outlook and caused him much pain: he could never believe in other people's sincerity. In each emotion he saw a fake. He also had a habit of piercing with his unusually sharp eyes through any one thus suspected.'

One cannot help recalling to one's mind Kitty's sincere

act of benevolence (under the influence of her friend Varenka: an up-to-date edition of Sonya), during her stay at a German Spa, and her subsequent self-reproaches because of it.

' "Oh, how stupid, how stupid! There was no need at all. . . . It was all pretence!" Kitty said, opening and shutting the sunshade.

' "But with what object?"

' "To appear better than others to myself and to God—to deceive everybody. No, I shall not give in to that again! Let me be bad, but at any rate not false, not a humbug!"

' "But who is a humbug?" asked Varenka reproachfully. "You speak as if . . ."

'But Kitty was in one of her fits of passion. She would not let Varenka finish.

' "I am not talking about you, not about you at all. You are perfection; but how can I help it if I am bad? It would not have happened if I were not bad. So let me be what I am, but not pretend. Let them live as they like, and I will live as I like. I cannot be different. . . . And it's all not the thing, not the thing!"

' "But what is not the thing?" said Varenka, quite perplexed.

' "It's all not the thing. I can't live except by my own heart, but you live by principle. I have loved you quite simply, but you, I expect, only in order to save me, to teach me."

These passages from *Anna Karenina* are worth quoting, because Tolstoy himself was more than familiar with the conflict between the sincerity of his heart (or his instincts), and that of his rules and principles. Wavering between them, he was inclined to doubt at times, like Kitty, the integrity of his own good actions. Thus, having organized the famine relief for the afflicted peasants in the Volga district, he suddenly made this entry in his diary, on May 23rd, 1893: 'Was at Begichevka. Felt indifference to the empty business of relief, and repulsion at the hypocrisy.' Even while planning, in the summer 1910, his flight from home, he wrote on July 21st: 'There is only one thing I want—to do not my will, but Thine.' To which he added as an afterthought: 'While writing thus, I ask myself, "Is it true? Am I posing to myself?" Help me, help me, help me!'

IV

Had there been a bridge between the irrational and the rational sides in Tolstoy's personality, his dilemma would have been simpler. On the other hand, the gap between the two provided a marvellous opportunity for Tolstoy the psychologist. It was mainly through observing and analysing himself that he obtained his wellnigh clairvoyant insight into human beings in general. But even here his attention was concentrated not so much on spiritual problems (these were tackled by his logic and reason) as on the psychological imponderables, preferably on those which camouflage the duplicity of human beings. As a debunker of appearances Tolstoy was in fact one of the most merciless realists—no matter whether he had recourse to amused contempt, as in his descriptions of Anna Sherer's salon (*War and Peace*), or to the cruel irony implied in the talk between Ivan Ilyitch's widow and his 'mourning' colleague about the pension.

But while remaining an enticing literary expedient, psychological analysis did nothing to alleviate Tolstoy's own dilemma. On the contrary, it increased his scepticism with regard to himself and human beings in general. This was not what he wanted. Unable to organize his complicated inner life, he had only one course left: to force it into a simplified mould, which he did as soon as the reasoning moralist in him had taken the upper hand.

Tolstoy's conversion thus resulted not in a higher synthesis of life, but only in a series of suppressions; in the dictatorship of self-imposed puritanic rules for the sake of which he was ready to cripple not only his own existence, but life as a whole. Yet human nature took its own—at least from time to time. Tolstoy's desperate asceticism, far from eradicating his full-blooded thirst for life, only made it more turbulent. Less than a year after his conversion he wrote to A. A. Fet: 'I am mad with living. . . . It is summer, the delicious summer. This year I have struggled for a long time; but the beauty of nature has conquered me. I rejoice in life.' Aylmer Maude tells us how, in the same year (1880), the aged Turgenev complained of his own relations to women. 'I had a love affair the other day,' he said, 'and would you believe it? I found it dull!' 'Ah,' exclaimed the converted Tolstoy, 'if only I were like that!'

Again in 1886 the Russian pianist Anton Rubinstein, whom Tolstoy ranked very high, was giving a concert in Moscow. As a lover of music, Tolstoy wished to hear Rubinstein's recital, but at the same time disapproved of it on moral grounds—it was a luxury for the rich. Lacerated by his inclinations and his ascetic 'rules', he yet confessed on the eve of the recital that he was sorry to miss the concert, as all the tickets had been sold out. Rubinstein heard of it and arranged an extra seat for Tolstoy who was glad to receive the invitation. Tolstoy set out to go to the recital, but sudden doubts assailed him as to whether he was doing the right thing. In the end his 'rules' won the battle. The consequence was a nervous attack of such severity that the doctor had to be called in.

In Gorky's shrewd *Reminiscences of Tolstoy* one finds some further examples of this kind. On one occasion, the anti-militarist Tolstoy walked together with Gorky in the streets of Moscow and saw in the distance two soldiers of the Guard. 'The metal of their accoutrements shone in the sun; their spurs jingled; they kept step like one man; their faces, too, shone with self-assurance of strength and youth. Tolstoy began to grumble at them: "What pompous stupidity! Like animals trained by the whip!" But when the guardsmen came abreast with him, he stopped, followed them with his eyes, and said enthusiastically: "How handsome! Old Romans, eh? What strength and beauty! O Lord! How fine it is when man is handsome, how very fine!" '

In the same work Gorky says of the old ascetic Tolstoy that, when he chose, he could be most simple and eloquent. But 'sometimes it was painful to listen to him. I always disliked what he said about women—it was unspeakably "vulgar", and at the same time very personal. The evening when I first got to know him, he took me to his study—it was at Khamovniki in Moscow—and, making me sit opposite to him, he began to talk about *Varenka Olessova* and *Twenty-Six and One*.[1] I was overwhelmed by his tone and lost my head; he spoke so plainly and so brutally, arguing that in a healthy girl chastity is not natural. . . . Then he began to speak about the girl in *Twenty-Six and One,* using a stream of indecent words with a simplicity which seemed to me cynical and even offended me.'

One could give many other illustrations of Tolstoy's duality which was painful and tragic for the very reason that each human feature assumed in him gigantic proportions: whether sympathy or egoism, the Epicurean joy of life or ascetic self-lacerations, the coldness of a rationalist or the impulsiveness of a child of Nature. Hence his inner tension, too, was bound to be on a much bigger, almost on a monstrous scale. Some further characteristics of this tension may perhaps help us to clarify our approach to Tolstoy's personality and work.

[1] Two of Gorky's well-known stories.

V

Culture and Nature

NO careful reader of Tolstoy can miss at least some of his affinities with Rousseau. Tolstoy himself admitted that as a boy he had idolized Rousseau and had even worn a medallion portrait of him instead of the orthodox cross. 'Many of his pages are so akin to me,' he said in a conversation, 'that it seemed to me I wrote them myself.' Both Tolstoy and Rousseau turned not only against the social order of their day, but against the entire civilization which they confused or even identified with sham-civilization. Both of them were driven by their propensities towards that primitive pattern of life which actually precedes what we call a cultured existence. Both showed a strong moralizing and educational vein. Moreover, having reached the climax of their fame, both of them wrote personal confessions with that frankness which—paradoxically enough—can become untruthful owing to its very exaggerations.

This was not mere coincidence. Tolstoy and Rousseau were at variance with their respective times largely because they were at variance with themselves. Their attacks on the period and the civilization to which they belonged were in essence flank attacks upon their own inner discord which they hoped to ease by a call to harmony and simplicity. Yet there is a world of difference between the primitive simplicity which knows no complexity, and the one which has overcome complexity. However much they resemble each other on the surface, they represent different levels of consciousness, of history, and of civilization. The harmony, symbolized by the legends of 'paradise' or of the 'golden age', points to that pre-individual (as well as pre-moral) wholeness which constitutes the main charm of primitive communities and also of children. On this plane the individual is still more or less merged with the collective group-psyche through which he participates in the life of the race and of Nature herself. Such *participation mystique,* or whatever its name, may be almost as instinctive as the life in a bee-hive. Not yet severed or differentiated from the group, the individual knows no disturbing problems and dilemmas of his own, but lives the life of the group. And so, whatever he does is right: no matter whether he hunts wild animals, paints beautiful ornaments on his weapons and utensils, or else slaughters the enemies of his tribe.

Yet had humanity stopped at this phase, it would have forfeited its history and growth. It would be in the position of a child refusing to leave his nursery and to develop into a youth and then into a man. The primitive Adam must taste of the Tree of Knowledge of good and evil; that is, he must commit the original sin of individuation, if he is to grow at all. There is no history, no progress, no civilization without the 'paradise lost'. This is a fact of enormous psychological and moral significance. For it means nothing less than the awakening of the individual and his assertion against the group. This differentiating process is accompanied by strife and division, by endless quest and suffering, until humanity is landed in a war of all against all, or even in mutual extermination. This does not mean, however, that such ought to be the outcome of history and civilization. Far from it. It means that only through its own Golgotha, resulting from individuation, can mankind mature and discover all its innate potentialities—good and evil.

The price itself may be terrible indeed, but having paid it fully humanity can arrive at a conscious sense of values, as well as at a free choice between them. Only after having broken up its passive pre-individual unity, can it hope to attain—through the process of individuation and the hell wrought by it—that new and integral unity which has overcome the conflicts inherent in the march of man and of civilization. Yet as long as the chaos and struggle last, nostalgia for the forfeited pre-individual 'paradise' or 'golden age' remains. Instead of accepting and overcoming the burden of civilization, many a person is anxious to avoid it, to run away from it—back to mankind's childhood, 'back to Nature'. Like Rousseau and like Tolstoy.

II

Tolstoy's call, 'back to Nature', was perhaps less sentimental but more complicated than that of Rousseau. And in spite of its masks and changes, it yet remained one of his basic features to the end of his life. It first came out in Tolstoy's spontaneous paganism, then in his sympathies for the peasant masses, and finally even in his Christian teaching the actual roots of which were hidden in some of the deepest recesses of his own unconscious. At the same time, it was at least partly conditioned also by the general background of the Russia Tolstoy had known in his youth and early manhood.

We must not forget that in Tolstoy's youth Russia was a vast feudal or semi-feudal country with little scope for the individual as such. Individual independence and initiative were hampered by the autocratic system, and even more by the too little differentiated peasant masses which, in some respects, were nearer to Asia than to Western Europe. In the passive and slumbering Asia the individual was still swallowed up, as it were, by the collective group-consciousness, while in the highly differentiated Europe individualism unbound was running riot at the expense of, or rather against, the group. Sandwiched between these two worlds lay Russia, one of her eyes turned to the East, and the other to the West.

Her gentry and higher aristocracy may have been more or less Europeanized, but her peasantry hardly differed much from the illiterate toiling masses anywhere in Asia. The gap between the two strata was both social and cultural, and it kept on growing. The 'intelligentsia' (a compound of impoverished noblemen and educated commoners) which, after the Crimean campaign, became the guardian of Russian culture, endeavoured to fill the gap, but in vain. The liberal and radical *narodniki* or populists actually adopted a kind of worship of the moujik, whom they often idealized beyond recognition. So did, for reasons of their own, the conservative Slavophils. Still, the masses repudiated both and persisted in their distrust of the gentlefolk. The isolated intellectuals thus felt more and more 'superfluous' in their own country. The problem was solved, and rather drastically, by the last revolution which discarded the old intelligentsia and the nobles in the name of a new classless society.

Tolstoy, with his hatred of the 'general tendency', kept aloof from any currents and movements, including the literary cult of the moujik. Yet no Russian author has ever been so irresistibly drawn towards the soil and the patriarchal peasant masses as Tolstoy. This was due above all to his organic rootedness in both. Born into a family of old aristocratic landowners, he regarded not only his estate, but also the serfs belonging to it as his proper background. He was so much tied to Yasnaya Polyana and to the beautiful central-Russian landscape around that he lived there—with a few unimportant interruptions—to the end of his days. Nor was this all. Economically speaking, the years of Tolstoy's youth and manhood coincided with the transition period between the agricultural feudal system and the new capitalist era in Russia. Such a transition was fraught, however, with obvious dangers to the landed gentry. The class to which Tolstoy belonged, gradually found itself compelled to face impoverishment, or else to hobnob with the moneyed bourgeoisie and the corrupt bureaucracy. In *War and Peace* we still see the gentry at the height of its power and prosperity. The foundations of the feudal system in Russia were not shaken even by Napoleon. A different age is represented, however, by *Anna Karenina.* This novel marks the period when, after the abolition of serfdom, both the gentry and the liberated peasants were threatened by the encroaching capitalism. The landowners, now dependent on hired labour, were compelled to adapt themselves to the new conditions if they did not want to be submerged by them. At all events they tried to be on good terms not only with the bureaucracy, but also with business. At the same time, a considerable portion of the village population was being gradually turned into town proletarians for the benefit of the new captains of industry. The old-world rural existence was thus passing through a crisis, and an ominous one.

A landowner himself, Tolstoy could not remain indifferent to such a state of things. The pattern of existence in which he was rooted and to which he owed his habits, tastes, and privileges, was at stake. So it was necessary to meet and to avert this danger. Once again Tolstoy rejected all half-measures. He wanted to undermine not only capitalism, but the very structure of life in which such a thing as capitalism was possible. And since our civilization is primarily of a capitalist order, he turned against the very idea of civilization. Let us go back to Nature, back to the soil! Let us all become primitive peasants rather than be drowned in the swamp of modern capitalism which spells nothing but ruin, universal egoism, and disintegration. Such was his slogan.

Tolstoy's moralizing and reformatory propensities must have been the more gratified by a campaign which was in full accord with his own rootedness in the ancestral soil and in the peasant masses belonging to it. In *War and Peace* the formula is not yet completely worked out, although its trend is indicated by the apotheosis of Platon Karatayev, the representative of the anonymous patriarchal peasantry. After all, it was not for nothing that the wealthy aristocrat Pierre Bezoukhov became so fascinated by him as to change his own orientation with regard to life. His criterion of good and evil was: in how far the peasant Karatayev would, or would not, approve of his doings. In *Anna Karenina,* again, the squire Levin, at the most crucial moment of his life, was saved by the wisdom of an illiterate peasant.

We need not reiterate the fact that in both Pierre Bezoukhov and Levin, Tolstoy gave us his own spiritual portrait. But not entirely. Certain features of his questioning and doubting self were projected by him into Prince Andrey Bolkonsky. While the Bolkonsky element in him stood for the proud and very self-conscious personality, the Karatayev element clamoured all the more for that warm and vegetative happiness which is inaccessible to an isolated individual. The working of these two incompatible yet simultaneous elements can be traced not only in Tolstoy's writings, but also in Tolstoy's life. The spontaneous child of Nature that was in him was all too often scrutinized and disturbed by the self-conscious questioner and maker of rules. The split was fundamental and so painful at times that eventually Tolstoy wanted to get rid of consciousness itself in order to get rid of the pain and isolation involved by it. Hence his instinctive cult of Karatayev and Karatayevism—a cult in which he remained consistent to the end of his life. As early as at the age of twenty he wrote in his diary: 'I will always assert that consciousness is the greatest moral evil that can befall a man.' And this is what he said more than forty years after (1890) in a letter to E. T. Popov: 'Individuality is weakness. In order to get rid of it we must find some purpose outside ourselves—we must forget ourselves in work (as one does when making boots, or ploughing), in the work of a whole life. Personality cannot be appeased. No sooner has it appeared than it begins to torment itself and to suffer.'

These two quotations can serve as a key to Tolstoy's main dilemma. Regarding the individual consciousness as 'the greatest moral evil', he was bound to reject for *moral* reasons the very idea of a civilization, based on individual assertion and differentiation. Dostoevsky wanted the human personality to develop to its utmost limits even if such a process should involve unspeakable pain and struggle. Tolstoy, on the other hand, found his own isolated personality so irksome at times that he wanted to run away from it—back to Karatayev and to the primitive collectives where the individual consciousness is still more or less dissolved in that of the group. Anything that fosters individualism at the expense of such collectives became anathema to him. All that was near to them attracted and fascinated him. His love for the patriarchal masses was the stronger because some of his own instincts had retained the impulsive freshness of the primitives. Uncle Eroshka in *The Cossacks* was nearer to him than the comrades belonging to his own social circle.

This inclination, or rather urge, was actually responsible for the trend of his reasoning. And since one of the 'general tendencies' of that period consisted in the cult of the individual, Tolstoy was the more determined to prove its fallacy. He rejected the individualist tendency not only on moral, but also on any other grounds, and even denied its function in history. His anti-individualistic philosophy of history in *War and Peace* is a proof. 'The movement of nations', he says there, 'is not produced by power, by mental activity, not even by a union of the two, as the historians have imagined, but by the activity of *all* men who take part in the event, and who are always connected with each other in such a way that those who take the greatest direct part in the event, assume the least responsibility and vice versa.' Tolstoy saw the only spring of historical happenings in the unconscious impulses and instincts of the masses. He even did his uttermost to represent Napoleon himself as an inflated puppet of those impulses; as a mere 'unconscious weapon for the working out of historical universal ends'.

It was not without an ulterior motive that Tolstoy contrasted Napoleon with the indolent and passive Kutuzov—the Russian generalissimo who dozed at the war councils, quietly leaving events to take care of themselves. Kutuzov, as portrayed by Tolstoy, realized that the important thing is not the individual but the Unconscious of the masses which a leader must follow rather than lead. True political and strategic wisdom consists in the obedience to the working of that collective Unconscious—such was Tolstoy's conclusion. He even stressed the fact that 'in historical events we see more plainly than ever the law of the Tree of Knowledge. It is only unconscious activity that bears fruit, and the man who plays a part in an historical drama never understands its significance. If he strives to comprehend it, he is striken with barrenness.'

Viewed from this angle, *War and Peace* can be called an epic of the mass-Unconscious, even if Tolstoy's interpretation of it does not go beyond a 'philosophy of collective fatalism', as one of his critics (Shelgunov) aptly called it. Is it then surprising that Count Pierre Bezoukhov found the wisdom of life in a primitive peasant who was the mouthpiece of that Unconscious, or of Nature herself? Also in Tolstoy's previous novel, *The Cossacks,* the civilized aristocrat Olenin fell in love with the half-savage Cossack *belle* Marianka, because she was like Nature. 'Maybe in her I love Nature,' mused Olenin. 'But I have not my own will, and through me an elementary force loves her, and the whole world, all Nature, impresses this love upon my soul, and says to me, "Love!" I love her not with my mind, not with my imagination, but with my whole being. Loving her, I feel myself an inseparable part of the whole blissful world.'

Tolstoy's leanings towards the undifferentiated masses and the group-consciousness of those masses was thus fostered by his own pantheistic nearness to Nature. Both were but the two aspects of one and the same basic urge which runs, like a thread or *leitmotif,* through most of his writings. The character of his own pantheism was clearly indicated even at the end of his early story *Luzern,* in which he says: 'There is one, but one sinless leader, the Universal Spirit, who penetrates us all as he does one and each separately, who imparts to each the tendency towards what is right; the same Spirit, who orders the tree to grow towards the sun, orders the flower to cast seeds in the autumn, and orders us to hold together unconsciously.' The imperative to 'hold together unconsciously', which sprang from Tolstoy's strongest inner urge, became in fact his own *daimonion.* It directed not only the trend of his artistic genius, but also his entire philosophy about morals, religion, and the meaning of life.

III

This imperative was the main reason of what might be called Tolstoy's one-track mind whenever he touched upon the problem of the individual and the group. All that threatened to destroy the unconscious compactness of the group, of the masses, was regarded by him as a moral evil and a crime against humanity. And since culture and civilization are unthinkable without differentiation, that is, without splitting up and destroying that compactness, Tolstoy could not help turning against all the aspects of civilized life. Nature versus Civilization; the mass-Unconscious versus the organized State; idyllic patriarchal conditions versus the artificiality and corruption of modern cities—such were some of Tolstoy's cardinal antitheses, prompted by his own *daimonion.* These determined the pattern and the method of his thinking which was one of black and white. Everything connected with civilization was bad—bad *a priori.* But all that came from 'Nature', from the compact patriarchal masses, could not be anything but good. Tolstoy may have suffered from a number of contradictions, yet on this point he remained consistent to the end. He never swerved from his conviction that the ideal of humanity was Karatayevism in all its manifestations. Gradually, he even went farther back, without shrinking from the most impossible conclusions. Thus in 1875 he wrote in a letter to Fet about his experiences among the primitive Bashkirs in the Samara steppes as follows: 'I had listened to the speeches in the British Parliament, which is considered very important, and it seemed to me dull and insignificant; but there [in the steppes] are flies, dirt, and Bashkir peasants, and I, watching them with respect and anxiety, became absorbed in listening to them, and felt it all to be very important.'

Only a man who had intimate personal reasons for clinging to such an attitude, could also defend that attitude with Tolstoy's one-sided ruthlessness. When the seeker Levin was on the verge of suicide, it never once entered his mind to look for an outlet among the learned Hamlet-like intellectuals of that period. He turned to the masses instead. And so did Tolstoy in an identical situation. 'I must seek the meaning not among those who have lost it and wish to kill themselves, but among those milliards of the past and present who make life and who support the burden of their own lives and of ours also,' he says in his *Confession*. 'And I considered the enormous masses of those simple, unlearned, and poor people who have lived and are living.' He did this not deliberately, but because he obeyed some of his profoundest instincts. Reason worked of course, as he says, but 'something else was also working which I can only call a consciousness of life. A force was working which compelled me to turn my attention to this and not to that; and it was this force which extricated me from my desperate situation and turned my mind in quite another direction.'

It is hardly necessary to repeat that this other direction was Tolstoy's 'back to Nature' trend. He fled to the impersonal group-consciousness in order to find in it his own personal salvation. If the individual self means pain, suffering, and isolation, then the quickest escape from it all leads through the refusal to have a self. So why not go back to the group, back to that universal 'holding together', in which Tolstoy saw the very essence of love, or of what he called love? Hence his dictum that 'love is love only when it is annihilation of one's individual self'. In his diary he even made (on June 30th, 1898) a dogmatic statement such as this: 'To many it seems that nothing will remain if you exclude personality from life and a love for it. It seems to them that without personality there is no life. But this only appears so to the people who have not experienced self-renunciation. Throw off personality from life, renounce it, and then there will remain that which makes the essence of life—love.' This precept can best be completed by the following passage, taken from one of his private letters: 'We talk of future life, of immortality. What is immortal is only what is not I. Love. God. Nature.'

Having identified the amorphous mass-consciousness with Love, God, and Nature, Tolstoy began to frame his own meaning of life accordingly. In this process he cut off without mercy everything that might undermine the compact pre-individual 'brotherhood' of men. And since he saw in culture and civilization the principal agents of division, he was morally bound to reject them wholesale. Referring (in a talk with the Russian pianist Goldenveizer) to Lichtenberg's aphorism that mankind will perish when not a single savage is left in the world, he once said with regret: 'I first turned to the Japanese, but they already have successfully adopted all the bad sides of our culture. The Kaffirs are the only hope left.' His fear of division and personal isolation made him utter the most extravagant things. In *The Kreutzer Sonata,* for example, he proclaimed, through his mouthpiece Poznyshov, all doctors as criminals—for the astonishing reason that during the epidemics the doctors isolate the infected 'brothers' from the rest of mankind. 'If you hearken to their counsels (so numerous and dangerous are the germs of disease that lurk in wait for you at every step you take), whatever you do will tend not to draw you closer to your fellow men, but to separate you from them more than ever. If the doctors' behests were faithfully carried out, every one of us should sit apart, completely isolated from everybody else, and would never think of putting the syringe with the carbolic acid out of his hand.'

Concurrently, he was always ready to exalt anything that took him away from culture and brought him closer to the folk-masses. In his admiration for these he often suppressed all critical judgment. Once he rated quite an average composition of a peasant boy higher than the works of Goethe. He also put Russian folk-songs above Beethoven whose ninth symphony he condemned on the ground that, being accessible only to the cultured *élite,* it fostered social disunion among men. In his pedagogic magazine, *Yasnaya Polyana,* he actually insisted that Beethoven and Pushkin please us not because of any artistic excellence, but because we, educated people, are as corrupt and perverted in our tastes as those two. His onslaught on Shakespeare (whom he ranked among the writers of the fourth order) is notorious. So is his pogrom on the entire modern art and literature, including his own novels. At least in theory, if not in practice, his final and only standard of excellence was in how far a work of art served as a vehicle of universal unity, compactness and selfless brotherhood among men. This was the one thing needed. All the rest was superfluous, and therefore harmful.

IV

What invariably strikes a reader of Tolstoy is the too frequent and too insistent a repetition of such *leitmotifs* as unity and brotherly love. It is so insistent, indeed, that in the end one suspects behind it more will to love than real love. Turgenev once said that Tolstoy had never loved anybody in our ordinary human sense, and he may have been right. The very scale of his split up personality and genius was one of the causes of his isolation in the midst of ordinary human beings. Hence his tendency to reduce that scale to the average, to less than the average. Tolstoy is a tragic example of a giant who became afraid of his own exceptional nature and wanted to throw off its burden by merging with the ordinary and the anonymous. But even here he went to extremes. And in order to convince himself that he—a Count by birth—was absolutely sincere in his striving after the Karatayev ideal, he began to imitate, in his later years, all that he considered typical of the Russian peasants.

In June 1881 he made a pilgrimage to the famous Optino monastery, on foot and in bast-shoes, like a peasant pilgrim. Whether he had the *naïveté* and spontaneity of a peasant's faith, is another question. His peasant blouse, the scythes and sickles in his study, or even his ploughing of the fields, are known to the world through Repin's paintings. Yet Tolstoy's efforts to simplify his life—like those of his Hindoo follower Gandhi—did not end here. Anna Seuron, a former governess in his family, tells us that in 1883 Count Tolstoy, already world-famous as a writer, suddenly began to take lessons in making boots. Once he appeared in high boots made by himself, and was very pleased with the compliments of his guests. He talked with enthusiasm about his new *métier* and even gave a demonstration in threading the waxen end, while sitting on a low bench and imitating his teacher. The same witness records that there was a time when he deliberately neglected his personal appearance and cleanliness—quite in the manner of the poorest peasant. 'He, who had always worn fine socks, suddenly demanded strips of linen, and began to wrap his feet in them as peasants do. . . . One day he announced that though lice, considered as insects, are dirty, yet a poor man should not be considered dirty for being lousy. Being poor, he is a natural prey to lice. To be clean requires means; it is a luxury.'

Quite a few of Tolstoy's simplifications bear the same sophisticated touch. Yet his will to be simple was genuine enough, even desperately so. The ideas which resulted from this, in the course of his reasoning, may not be of great interest as philosophy. Psychologically, however, they are important. At least in so far as they give a clue to some of his inner conflicts the nature of which was further complicated by his irrational fear of death.

VI

The 'Dragon of Death'

IN spite of his vexation of spirit, Tolstoy the man, or rather Tolstoy the pagan, was brimming over with vitality, with passion and the joy of life. His love of life was immense and organic. When free from the interference of his moralizing double, he could abandon himself to each passing experience with an intensity and intoxication which seemed to challenge the flow of time itself. But time could neither be defied nor stopped. Its flow continued, one moment annihilating the other—a ceaseless process of death. And if so, was not life itself with all its joy, passions, and beauty only a delusion? Not a fact to be indulged in, but a problem to be solved? A problem, inseparable from the problem of death on the one hand, and from that of personality on the other. Does death mean a complete destruction of one's life and one's self? Or is it merely a mutation, a passage to another plane of existence? And where is any guarantee which could offer us a prospect beyond utter annihilation and oblivion?

Caught in the whirl of questions without answers, Tolstoy with all his untamed vitality was in the end certain of one thing only: that death followed him, like an executioner, turning his existence into a slow process of dying the symptoms of which kept on growing all the time. 'Life flows,' he complains in his *Confession*. 'And what does it mean? Life flows—means: one's hair falls out, becomes grey; one's teeth decay; wrinkles, bad smell in the mouth. Even before everything is finished, it assumes a dreadful, repulsive appearance;

one notices the layers of rouge and powder, perspiration, stench, deformity. And where is that which I served? Where is beauty? . . . There is no beauty—there is nothing. There is no life. Apart from the fact that there is no life in that in which there seemed to be life, you yourself begin to drift away from it, to get weaker, uglier; you rot away, others snatch away from you those pleasures in which you found your happiness of existence.'

It was not so much the metaphysical as the physical and biological fear of death that overwhelmed him with a despair which was really nothing else but his inverted and full-blooded love of happiness and of life. Unable to justify death before life, he was compelled to put up with the fact of death as his permanent bogy and nightmare. 'There is nothing worse than death,' he wrote, quite in the spirit of a pagan, on October 17th, 1860, to the poet Fet. 'And when you properly think that with it everything comes to an end, then there is nothing worse than life either.' In August 1869 Tolstoy travelled from Nizhny Novgorod (now Gorky) to the Penza district and stayed overnight in the little town of Arzamas. Unable to sleep, he was suddenly overwhelmed by such a fear of death as verged on madness. Fifteen years later, he recorded that experience in his unfinished *Memoirs of a Madman*—a valuable document for a proper understanding of Tolstoy. His gradual orientation towards death was all the more crushing because of his enormous vitality. It was the vitality of a materialist who secretly believed only in this world and was sceptical of any 'beyond', while knowing full well that everything existing in this world is doomed to perish. The very exuberance of his joy of life thus turned against itself. It degenerated into hatred of life, into negation and despair.

'I looked on all the works that my hands had wrought, and on the labour that I laboured to do: and behold, all was vanity and vexation of spirit, and there was no profit for them under the sun. And I turned to myself to behold wisdom, and madness, and folly. . . . But I perceived that one event happened to them all. Then said I in my heart, as it happeneth to the fool, so it happeneth even to me, and why was I then more wise? Then I said in my heart, that this also is vanity. For there is no remembrance of the wise more than of the fool for ever; seeing that which now is in the days to come shall be forgotten. And how dies the wise man? As the fool. Therefore I hated life. . . . This is an evil in all that is done under the sun, that there is one event unto all. . . . For the living know that they shall die: but the dead know not anything, neither have they any more a reward; for the memory of them is forgotten. Also their love, and their hatred, and their envy, is now perished; neither have they any portion for ever in any thing that is done under the sun.'

This is what life can seem like from the angle of death. Had Solomon (or whoever wrote those lines) been a less full-blooded individual, his despair too would have been smaller. An ordinary respectable mortal does not even condescend to being troubled by such problems. His very indifference is a safeguard against them. So are the ready-made formulae offered by official religions. No such solutions were, however, acceptable to Tolstoy. He preferred to grope at his own risk for an outlet of his own. And the results at which he arrived can again best be studied in his works.

II

There is hardly another great author in whose writings the death-theme plays so conspicuous a part as in Tolstoy. Even the serene flow of his *Childhood* is disturbed by death. The bubbling life in *The Cossacks* is darkened by the agony of the mortally wounded Lukashka. His Sebastopol stories are full of it. And as for *War and Peace,* death hovers over some of its finest chapters. While entertainments run their course in the aristocratic salons of both capitals, the old grandee,

Count Bezoukhov, is dying—lonely, numb, and helpless—in his Moscow palace. The death of Prince Andrey's young wife is shown in all its realism. So is, later on, the protracted agony of Prince Andrey himself—to mention only a few cases. In a memorable chapter in *Anna Karenina* we see the arrival of Levin's consumptive brother, bringing with him the atmosphere of death and the dying. The pages dealing with the last days of his life are as incisive as the description of Anna's suicide. It would hardly be possible to tell of a more terrifying agony than the one in *The Death of Ivan Ilyitch.* And Tolstoy's early story, *Three Deaths,* is based on the parallelism between the death of an old lady, a dying peasant, and a felled birch tree.

The very idea of such a comparison was characteristic of Tolstoy. He scrutinized them, one after the other, in order to find out which of the three was the easiest, and why. The conclusion he arrived at was simple: the more primitive the consciousness, the easier the death. The spoilt and civilized upper-class lady dies amidst incredible sufferings. The peasant—a primitive child of Nature—passes away without fear or worry. Easiest of all, however, is the death of the tree which, being inanimate, is devoid of consciousness. But this is how Tolstoy himself defends his theme in a letter (May 1st, 1858) to Countess Alexandra Tolstaya: 'Here we reach a point where we disagree about my story. You are wrong in judging it from a Christian angle. My idea was this: three beings die—a lady, a peasant, a tree. The worldly lady is pitiable and wretched, since she lived surrounded by lies and dies surrounded by them. Christianity, as she understands it, does not solve for her the problem of life and death. Why should she die at all, since she wants to live? Her mind and imagination make her believe in the promised life beyond, yet her entire being protests, because she knows no solace (except that offered by her false Christianity). Hence she is wretched and pitiable. The peasant dies in peace, and he does so precisely because he is not a Christian. He keeps by habit to Christian observances, yet his religion is a different one; it is the religion of Nature amidst which he lives. With his own hands he fells trees, mows, slaughters and breeds sheep as naturally as children are born and old men die; he knows this law of nature and has never turned away from it, as the old lady has done; he sees nature face to face. "An animal", you will say, and why not? Is there anything wrong with it? An animal represents beauty and happiness, and harmony with the whole universe, and not discord with it, like the old lady. The tree dies calmly in freedom and beauty, because it knows no falsity, no distortions, no fears and regrets. Such is my idea of which, I am sure, you will not approve. But it would be futile to argue: it is in your soul, and in mine too.'

Tolstoy's personal encounters with death only helped to increase his preoccupation with its mystery and horror. The most crushing of them all was the death of his consumptive brother Nicholas at Hyères, in 1860. Its details are recorded in *Anna Karenina*. Yet its immediate effect on Tolstoy can be gathered also from his correspondence. Thus, a month after the funeral, he wrote to Fet: 'I presume you know what has happened. On the 20th September he died, literally in my arms. Nothing in my life has ever made such an impression upon me. He was right in saying that there is nothing worse than death. And once a man has realized that death is the end of everything, then there is nothing worse than life either. . . . A few minutes before he died he fell into a doze, then suddenly awoke and murmured with horror, "But what is all this?" He must have seen it, this absorption of oneself into nothing. And if he found no support, how could I hope to find it? . . . Of what use is anything, since the agonies of death will come to-morrow, with all the abomination of self-delusion and falsehood, and since everything will end in nothing, in absolute nought for oneself. . . . Of course, as long as there is a desire to know and to tell the truth, one tries to know and tell it. This is all that is still left to me of the moral world, higher than that I cannot place myself. And this alone I will do, but not in the form of your art. Art is a lie, and I can no longer love a beautiful lie.'

Tolstoy was only thirty-two when writing this letter. Nevertheless, the last few lines anticipate the Tolstoy of *Confession,* of *What is Art,* and of his moralizing pamphlets. From that time on the shadow of death never left him. It cast a spell over him, against which he was helpless. To make matters worse, only in the course of 1874–5 five people died in his house at Yasnaya Polyana—among them two of his own children. What his personal reactions to it were like can be judged by certain pages of his *Confession,* as well as by his private letters and diaries. From these one can moreover conclude that he was as much of a sceptic and unbeliever as any Russian intellectual of that period. So he had to work out an emergency faith of his own simply in order to ward off the 'dragon of death', mentioned in his Eastern fable. This was not an easy task. And the mood behind it can perhaps be gauged by the avowal, jotted down by Tolstoy less than a month after his brother's death: 'During the funeral itself, the thought came to me to write a materialistic gospel, the life of Christ—as a materialist.'

III

A considerable portion of Tolstoy's creations can be defined as a duel with death. In his early period he wrote in order to affirm life even in the face of death. His later works, however, resemble a continuous effort to exorcise the bogy of death, or to make it at least bearable. The approximate turning-point (but not a breaking-point) between these two phases was his *Confession,* on the very first pages of which he acknowledges the nature of this impasse. 'It was impossible to stop, impossible to go back, and impossible to close my eyes or avoid seeing that there was nothing ahead but suffering and real death—complete annihilation. . . . One can only live while one is intoxicated with life; as soon as one is sober it is impossible not to see that it is all mere fraud and a stupid fraud! . . . I cannot now help seeing day and night going round and bringing me to death. That alone I see, for that alone is true. All else is false.'

Confronted thus with Solomon's dilemma, Tolstoy first inquired into the resources offered to him by philosophy, science, the Church. It was all in vain. The bogy refused to be exorcised. And like Levin in *Anna Karenina,* he, too, found in the end not a real solution, but only a shelter. This was provided by his going back to the primitives, to a past stage of consciousness. Both were 'saved' by the Christian way of life which they had discovered among the ignorant peasants. The only difference being that Tolstoy tried to construe it into a system of rules which should be valid not only for him, but for all men. It was, in short, his *daimonion* which helped him out by urging him to return to the 'aggregate of personalities'; to merge his tormented personal self with the consciousness of a primitive collective just as a drop of water dissolves in the sea, or a Buddhist in Nirvana. He even found in this shelter a substitute for Nirvana, of which, incidentally, he had considerable theoretical knowledge. In the summer of 1869 he studied the works of Schopenhauer and even contemplated translating them. He did not hesitate to proclaim him (in a letter to Fet, dated August 30th, 1869) the greatest of geniuses. Besides, Tolstoy had displayed his own enthusiasm for Nirvana much earlier: in Prince Andrey's soliloquy on the battlefield of Austerlitz (*War and Peace*).

When the mortally wounded Prince Andrey had recovered his senses, the first thing he became aware of was the sky—the 'lofty sky, not clear, but still immeasurably lofty, with grey clouds creeping quietly over it. "How quietly, peacefully, and triumphantly, and not like us, running, shouting, and fighting, not like the Frenchmen and artillerymen dragging the mop from one another with frightened and frantic faces, how different are those clouds creeping over that lofty, limitless sky! How was it I did not see that lofty sky before? And how happy I am to have found it at last. Yes! All is vanity, all is false, except that infinite sky. There is nothing, nothing but that. But even that is not; there is nothing but peace and stillness. And thank God!" ' . . . Even his former ideal, the great individualist Napoleon, now seemed to him petty and trifling. Gazing at the victorious Corsican who happened to pass by, Prince Andrey mused on the nothingness of greatness, on the nothingness of life, of which no one could comprehend the significance, and on the nothingness—still more—of death, the meaning of which could be understood and explained by none of the living. It was weariness and resignation in which the Nirvana-mentality shone with all its seductive glow. And Tolstoy himself was falling in love with that glow. In another letter to Fet (in 1872) he frankly stressed that 'in Nirvana there is nothing to laugh at; still less is there cause for anger. We all (I at least) feel that it is much more interesting than life; but I agree that however much I may think about it, I can think of nothing else than that Nirvana is nothingness. I only stand for one thing: religious reverence—awe before that Nirvana. At any rate, there is nothing more important than it.'

The entire second half of Tolstoy's life was marked by a 'religious reverence' and worship of his own home-made Nirvana. This was why he canonized the group-consciousness into a divine status: the command of 'brotherly love' on that pre-individual plane was identified by him with God Himself. The need to drown his own self in such 'love' increased at the same rate as did his inner doubts and torments. He hoped to get rid of them, as well as of his bogy, by dissolving his (or any) personality in the amorphous mass. This became not an active principle with him, but a kind of spiritual drug from which he expected an alleviation of his pain, as certain people expect it from alcohol. 'In order to save oneself, i.e. in order not to be unhappy and suffering, one must forget oneself', we read in his diary (December 25th, 1894). 'The only way of doing this is to forget oneself through love, but the majority of people succumb to temptations, and neither like nor wish to forget themselves by means of love, but endeavour to forget themselves by means of tobacco, wine, opium, arts.'

This strange avowal is valuable as a psychological clue to Tolstoy's teaching, and also as another proof that the most 'selfless' love can often be dictated by impulses whose primary aim is one's selfish inner comfort. Tolstoy did not seem to be perturbed by this aspect of his doctrine. On the contrary, he extolled it, and even discovered in it a safeguard against the bogy of death. In *What I Believe* he stated frankly that one should live for others, and only for others, because of the immediate personal benefit derived from such impersonal love. 'Death, death, death awaits you every second. Your life passes in the presence of death. If you labour personally for your own future, you yourself know that the one thing awaiting you is—death. And that death ruins all you work for. Consequently, life for oneself can have no meaning. If there is a reasonable life it must be found elsewhere; it must be a life the aim of which does not lie in preparing life for oneself. To live rationally one must live so that death cannot destroy life.' He is even more explicit in his book, *On Life,* where he says: 'If a man could place his happiness in the happiness of other beings, that is, if he would love them more than himself, then death would not represent to him that discontinuance of happiness and life, such as it does represent to a man who lives only for himself. Death, to the man who lived only for others, could not seem to be a cessation of happiness and life, because the happiness and life of other beings is not only not interrupted with the loss of life of a man who saves them, but is frequently augmented and heightened by the sacrifice of his life.'

In a word: the self is nothing, the group is everything. The only possible salvation for the isolated individual lies in his disappearance in the pre-individual group-consciousness through 'love'. Tolstoy even called it Christian love, although Christ did not insist that we should love our neighbours *more* than ourselves. Perhaps, because the *right kind* of love for oneself is by no means an easy matter; it can indeed be much more difficult, at times, than loving others. What merit is there in 'universal love' if this is only a camouflaged flight from oneself—a flight from which one, moreover, expects personal dividends? The dividends demanded by Tolstoy were certainly not trifling, as we can see from the following entry in his diary (July 13th, 1896): 'Christianity does not give happiness, but safety; it lets you down to the bottom from which there is no place to fall.' A few weeks earlier (May 17th) he was even more explicit when writing that 'to him who lives a spiritual life entirely, life here becomes so uninteresting and burdensome that he can part with it easily'.

IV

Unable to cope with the 'dragon of death' in any other way, Tolstoy was anxious to forget himself through what he called love. He took the line of least resistance by trying to lower his consciousness to a plane which humanity has left behind. His 'back to Nature' call and his 'Christian love' thus converged and actually blended. This is why Tolstoy's Rousseauism was, in some of its aspects, more radical and more uncompromising than anything Rousseau ever taught. His sympathy for the compact uncivilized masses, as well as his hatred of anything that threatened to disrupt them, had its roots in Tolstoy's personal phobias, the clues to which are amply provided by his works.

What fascinated him in the patriarchal Russian peasantry and in the 'primitives' in general, was above all the absence of those fears and torments from which he himself suffered. And he suffered the more because his elemental feeling of life was that of a primitive, while his mind was that of a destructive up-to-date sceptic. Unable to take anything for granted, not even his innate joy of life, he questioned and eventually undermined everything. With his back against the wall, he could not possibly have hoped to find an answer to his quest among the thinking and the learned, since most of them were as sceptical as he himself. So he was bound to turn to those who do not brood and think, but are guided by instincts. The point of view, so significantly indicated in *Three Deaths,* thus remained Tolstoy's cardinal attitude also later on. It could be put as follows: if a highly developed consciousness involves suffering, then we can cease to suffer only by 'simplifying' our consciousness, i.e. by reducing it to a more primitive level. We must learn, not from those who are in the same painful position as ourselves, but from those who know the secret of vegetative happiness. As Tolstoy himself puts it in his *Confession*: 'In contrast to us, who the wiser we are the less we understand the meaning of life, and see some evil irony in the fact that we suffer and die, these folk live and suffer, and they approach death and suffering with tranquillity and in most cases gladly. In contrast to the fact that a tranquil death, a death without horror and despair, is a very rare exception in our circle, a troubled, rebellious, and unhappy death is the rarest exception among the people. And such people, lacking all that for us is the only good of life and yet experiencing the greatest happiness, are a great multitude.'

Having thus discovered that shelter from which he could 'approach death and suffering with tranquillity', he insisted on his new gospel with a vehemence equal only to the danger on the part of his own lurking unbelief. It was among the primitive masses that he found that safe 'bottom from which there is no place to fall'. And the discovery struck him as being momentous enough to deserve the status of a new religion.

VII

Tolstoy and Religion

IT is important to remember that neither Tolstoy's conversion nor his Christian convictions came to him all of a sudden. Both kept on fermenting in him through a long and often confusing process, the initial stages of which can easily be traced back to his youth. Even the idea of becoming the founder of a religion had stirred up his mind as far back as his twenties. 'A conversation about divinity has suggested to me a great, a stupendous idea, to the realization of which I feel myself capable of devoting my life,' he wrote in his diary during the Crimean campaign. 'This idea is the founding of a new religion corresponding to the present state of mankind: the religion of Christianity, but purged of dogmas and mysticism; a practical religion not promising future bliss, but giving bliss on earth. I understand that to accomplish this the conscious labour of generations will be needed. One generation will bequeath the idea to the next, and some day fanaticism or reason will accomplish it. Deliberately to promote the union of mankind by religion—that is the basic thought which, I hope, will dominate me.

It soon dominated him almost to the exclusion of everything else. The impulse to 'promote the union of mankind' became his basic urge, his *daimonion* which, step by step, determined even the direction of his reasoning. The outcome was what might be called Tolstoy's religious teaching. Prompted by entirely irrational motives, this teaching turned in the end so rational indeed that each of its articles of faith had to pass through the severest scrutiny on the part of his logic and reason. In this way he reduced religion itself to a system of moral rules, based on his own interpretation of Christ's Gospel, or rather of the Sermon on the Mount. It was a static and uninspiring system. Even his conversion—in so far as it was a conscious process—showed no spontaneity, nothing of God's Grace. On the surface, at any rate, it was the outcome not of religious *élan,* but of a protracted logical travail.

He himself confessed that much to Countess Alexandra Tolstaya during his most critical period. This is what he wrote to her in April 1876: 'I was happy to learn your opinion (if I understood it rightly) according to which conversion rarely occurs instantaneously, but that pain and suffering are on its path. I was happy, because I myself have gone through a long and painful inner labour. I know that these pains and sufferings are the best I have experienced so far in my life and that they must have their reward, if not in the soothing quiet of faith, then at least in the awareness of the price I paid for them. The theory that God's Grace descends upon one, in the English clubs or in an assembly of stockbrokers, I always considered not only stupid, but also immoral. You say you do not know in what I myself believe. Strange and terrible to say: I believe in nothing, in nothing that is being taught by religion, and at the same time I not only hate, but despise unbelief. I don't see how one can live and still less how one can die without faith. I am gradually constructing my own beliefs, yet however firm I may be about them, they are not very firm and not very consoling. When my reason questions, their answer is satisfactory; but when my heart suffers and needs an answer, it receives from them neither support nor comfort. The demands of my reason and the answers given by the Christian religion could be compared with two hands anxious to join each other but whose fingers refuse to do so. I am craving for their union, but the more I try to join them, the worst it gets. Yet I know that it can be done and that they are made for one another.'

In February 1877 (that is, during his *Anna Karenina* period) he was even more outspoken about his state of mind, when to the same correspondent he bluntly acknowledged that for him religion was a question of a drowning man who looks for something to clutch to in order to avoid going to the bottom. While seeing in religion the only saving plank, he was yet unable to believe, unless he forced himself to do so. 'If you ask me what it is that prevents me from floating on the surface with the board, I will not tell you, because I am afraid of disturbing your faith, and I know that faith is one's greatest boon. I also know that you will smile at the idea that my doubts could disturb you. Still, it is important to know, not which of us reasons better, but what should be done to save one from drowning. This is why I will not talk to you about them; on the contrary, I shall be glad for you and all those who are floating in the little boat that does not carry me. I have a good friend, the savant Strakhov, one of the best men I know. We both agree considerably in our ideas about religion; we agree that philosophy cannot help us, that without religion we cannot live, yet neither of us can believe. This year we are both going to the Optino Monastery. There I will explain to the monks all the reasons why I cannot believe.'

II

All the world knows how Tolstoy turned for help to the simple faith of the masses 'sustaining life'. But in spite of his powerful instincts, he was too much of an intellectual to be able to embrace the moujiks' faith uncritically and without the sanction of logic. So he laboured towards a creed of his own which would correspond to the Christianity of the masses and at the same time be completely acceptable to his logic and reason. The result was a strange mixture of

Karatayev (or rather of the old peasant Akim in *The Power of Darkness*) on the one hand, and of a thorough-going eighteenth-century rationalist on the other. He took from the Gospel only the 'useful' Sermon on the Mount, and even this he reduced to five bald rules: do not be angry; do not commit adultery; do not take oaths; do not resist evil; be no man's enemy! As though anxious to appease his own sceptical reason, he sifted the Gospel through his intellect in such a way as to eliminate from it any taint of mysticism. He himself stressed in a private letter that the 'business of religion is like geometry. Religion is not composed of a conglomerate of words which may well act upon the people; religion is composed of simple, apparent, clear, indubitable moral truths, which are separated from the chaos of false and deceptive judgments; and such are the truths of Christ.'

Having thus identified religion with morality, Tolstoy immediately set out to separate the 'simple, clear, indubitable' moral truths and rules from the 'chaos of false and deceptive judgments'. And his ultimate criterion was dictated almost exclusively by his own hostility towards individualism, that is, by his longing for that primitive harmony which rests on simplification and exclusion rather than on integration. Instead of integrating his own turbulent instincts and passions, for example, he only put a 'chain' on them. Although broadminded and truly universal as an artist, Tolstoy turned into a kind of narrow-minded sectarian as soon as he began to preach his own version of the Sermon on the Mount. And after 1880 he preached it without ceasing: by means of pamphlets, private talks, letters, and even literary works proper.

The disturbing point about it all was that from behind Tolstoy's own Christianity there continued to peer such bald and utilitarian rationalism as to outstrip any 18th-century deist. Christ as a living personality simply did not exist for him. What he was concerned with, were only Christ's 'rules' which he would readily have taken from any other source, as long as it suited his purpose. 'I have no predilection whatever for Christianity,' he wrote in 1909 to the Polish painter Jan Styka. 'I owe my particular interest in the doctrine of Jesus: first, to the fact that I was born in that religion and lived among the Christians; secondly, to the great spiritual joy which I found in the process of freeing that pure doctrine from the astonishing falsifications wrought by the Churches.' His aversion to the 'general tendency' asserted itself here, too, in full measure. Some of his attacks upon the official Churches were unequalled in ferocity. So was his jeering at the mystical symbols of the Christian religion. (The most notorious and rather cheap specimen of this kind is his description of the Orthodox Church service in *Resurrection.*) In *The Kingdom of God is Within You* he actually stressed the fact that the Nicene Creed must lose all value for a man who has accepted the Sermon on the Mount, and vice versa. Taking religious symbols but on the plane of the reasoning logic, he was anxious to weed out not only what is beneath logic, but also what may be above or beyond it. In this manner he turned Christ Himself into a Tolstoyan.

At the same time he developed a peculiar dogmaticism and intolerance of his own. His moral system soon became a strait-jacket which he wanted to impose upon the whole of life. Anything that went beyond that strait-jacket was denounced without mercy. Yet the very firmness of Tolstoy's own dogmas is enough to put one on one's guard. A closer scrutiny can actually detect a triple fear behind it all: his fear of doubt, of the flesh, and of death. A rational shelter from it was provided by his 'rules' and a more effective irrational one—by his 'religious reverence' of Nirvana which urged him to dissolve and disappear in the compactness of the group-consciousness. A test case was Tolstoy's attitude towards the immortality of the soul. Whereas Dostoevsky, with his dynamic spiritual life, was driven nearly mad by the idea of personal extinction after death, Tolstoy accepted such a possibility with scarcely disguised enthusiasm. He welcomed it as a boon which may rid us of the tormented personal self for ever.

'Belief in personal immortality always seems to me a misunderstanding,' Tolstoy said in 1896 to the pianist Goldenveizer. In *What I Believe* he even called it a superstition. 'We are convinced that this superstition is something very elevated, and seriously try to prove the superiority of our teaching to other doctrines by the fact that we hold this superstition, while others, such as Chinese and Hindoos do not hold it. . . . Christ, in contradistinction to temporal, private personal life, teaches that eternal life, which, in Deuteronomy, God promised to Israel; with this difference, that, according to the Jewish conception, eternal life endured only in the chosen people of Israel; while, by Christ's teaching, eternal life continues in the Son of Man; and what is needed to preserve it, is the observance of the laws of Christ, which express God's will for the whole of humanity. Christ contrasts with personal life, not a life beyond the grave, but common life bound up with the past, present and the future life of the whole of humanity, the life of the Son of Man. . . . Moses' service of God is a service of the God of one people, while Christ's service of God is a service of the God of all mankind.'

In plain words: whereas the Jewish God is the apotheosis of the group-soul of a single race or nation, the Christian God (as Tolstoy interprets him) is a canonization of the group-soul or group-consciousness of the entire humanity—depersonalized and reduced to an amorphous mass, held together by what Tolstoy calls love. 'The whole teaching of Christ,' he goes on, 'is that his disciples, having understood the illusory nature of personal life, should renounce it and transfer it into the life of the whole of humanity; the life of the Son of Man. The teaching of the immortality of one's personal soul, on the other hand, does not call for the renunciation of one's personal life, but rivets that personality for ever. . . . Any meaning given to a personal life, if it be not based on the renunciation of self for the service of man, humanity, the Son of Man, is a delusion which flies to pieces at the first contact with reason. That my personal life perishes and that the life of the whole world in the will of the Father does not perish, and that only by merging with it can I possibly be saved, of that I can have no doubt. But this is so little in comparison with those exalted religious beliefs in a future life! Though it be little, it is sure. . . . I know that there is no other exit for me or for all those who, together with me, are tormented in this life. . . . I am not frightened about whether I shall have more unpleasantness or whether I shall die sooner. This may be terrible to one who does not see how senseless and ruinous is his separate, personal life, and who thinks he will not die. But I know that my life, aiming at personal solitary happiness, is the greatest absurdity, and that at the end of this stupid life there is inevitably nothing but a stupid death. I shall die like every one else, like those who do not fulfil the teaching; but, both for me and for all, my life and death will have a meaning. My life and death will serve the salvation of all, and that is what Christ taught.'

III

Utterances such as these reveal the escapist kernel of Tolstoy's 'Christian' teaching. It was a Buddhistic flight from himself: from his loneliness, his torments, his biological fear of death. Instead of achieving the highest realization of his own self by making it include the whole of humanity, he wanted it to dissolve and disappear in the latter. And he did his utmost to confer upon such flight from individualism a religious halo. Equally anti-Christian is his acceptance of the law of Karma, that is, of automatic moral retribution, independent of the existence or non-existence of God.

Tolstoy was full of praise when extolling the happiness and bliss conferred upon him by his new faith. Yet neither his self-assurance nor his public utterances should be taken at their face value. His private diaries, or at least those in which he spoke only to himself and not to posterity, testify to a less blissful state of mind. Thus on October 4th, 1897, that is, eighteen years after his conversion, he wrote: 'Not long ago, in the summer, I felt God for the first time; that He existed and that I existed in Him; in Him, like a limited thing in an unlimited thing, in Him also like a limited being in which He existed.' And in brackets: 'Horribly bad, unclear. But I felt it clearly and especially keenly for the first time in my life.' Well and good. But if this was for the *first* time in his life, we are entitled to ask how was it possible for him to preach with such certainty, during all those eighteen years, about God, God's Kingdom, Law and Will? Moreover, only a few months after his first experience of God, he made this perplexing entry (on July 17th, 1898): 'An inner struggle. I believe little in God. I do not rejoice at the examination, but am burdened by it, admitting in advance that I won't pass. All last night I did not sleep. I rose early and prayed much.'

This lack of faith was a secret which he was anxious to hide from others and particularly from himself. Tormented by doubts, by uncertainty, he therefore insisted all the more on the absolute validity of those Christian precepts which he himself had chosen and proclaimed as universal truths. What mattered to him was peace: peace within and without. As a weary man yearns for the days of childhood, Tolstoy yearned for the childhood of humanity whose undifferentiated pre-individual psyche allured him like a haven of peace. And in order to make this peace final, Tolstoy wanted mankind to go back to such external conditions as would perpetuate that static Kingdom of God (as he called it) for ever. To quote his own words, 'the whole of Christ's teaching consists in giving the Kingdom of God, that is peace, to man. In the Sermon on the Mount, in the talk of Nicodemus, in his charge to his disciples, and in all his sermons, Christ speaks only of the things that divide men and hinder them from being at peace and entering the Kingdom of God. . . . Men need only trust Christ's teaching, and obey it, and there will be peace on earth; and not a peace as men devise, temporary, accidental, and partial, but a general peace, inviolable and eternal.'

The urge towards peace and happiness, as defined above, was Tolstoy's inner voice: the voice of his conscience and, therefore, of conscience in general. All that mankind has got to do is to listen to the voice of conscience and act accordingly. And if personality with all its appetites is the chief obstacle on the path to peace, then personality itself should be destroyed—both psychologically and metaphysically. Let us go 'back', only much farther than Rousseau ever dreamt of! Let us return to that level of consciousness where history and civilization are impossible! Both of them involve pain, strife, division and self-division, and what is the good of it? Mankind will taste of true bliss only if it takes the shortest cut back to that state in which separate individuals are sacrificed to the amorphous group and where depersonalizing 'Christian' love is a natural condition.

IV

Springing from the depths of his wishful thinking, Tolstoy's Christianity was thus directed against the central Christian idea: the idea of the absolute worth, independence, and inner freedom of every human personality. Tolstoy must have been only too familiar with Pascal's *le moi est haïssable*. Hence his anxiety to escape from it into what he called brotherly love. And the more 'brotherly' it was, the pleasanter was the inner relief derived from it. At a moment of perfect frankness he even identified (in his diary) love towards one's enemies with spiritual voluptuousness. 'Love towards one's enemies. . . . What happiness, once you have attained it! There is an exquisite sweetness in this love, even in the foretaste of it. And this sweetness is just in the inverse ratio to the attractiveness of the object of love. Yes, the spiritual voluptuousness of love towards one's enemies.'

The passage is almost suggestive of a spiritual *gourmet*. But this was not all. A striking feature of Tolstoy's *ersatz*-religion was his promise of comfort on the cheapest possible terms. In *What I Believe* he even exhorted humanity to embrace his own version of Christian teaching on the ground that the position of Christ's followers is more profitable than any other. 'To verify this,' he argued, 'let every one remember all the painful moments of his life, all the physical and spiritual sufferings he has endured and still endures, and ask himself for what has he borne all these misfortunes, for the sake of the world's teaching, or for that of Christ's? Let every sincere man remember well his whole life and he will see that never, not once, has he suffered from obeying the teaching of Christ, but that most of the misfortunes of his life have come about because, contrary to his own inclination, he has followed the world's teaching which constrained him. . . . Christ does not call us to something worse instead of something better, but to something better instead of something worse. He pities people who appeared to Him like lost sheep, perishing without a shepherd and good pasture. He does not say that by following His teaching they will suffer more than by following the world's teaching; on the contrary, He says that those who will follow the teaching of the world will be unhappy and those who follow His teaching will be blessed. Christ does not teach salvation by faith or by asceticism—that is, by a deception of imagination or by voluntarily tormenting oneself in this life; but He teaches life in which, besides salvation from the loss of personal life, there will, here in this world, be less of suffering and more of joy than by a personal life. Christ, revealing His teaching, says that there is true worldly advantage in not taking thought for the worldly life.'

This 'worldly advantage' may not be objectionable in itself. Yet when it is used as a bait on behalf of a religious and moral life, it acquires a bad odour. Religion, as long as it is worthy of its name, cannot be degraded to a haggling for 'good pastures', worldly comforts and advantages. Once it has renounced spiritual heroism for the sake of a catalogue of profitable rules, it has ceased to be religion. Tolstoy's weakness in this respect compares very unfavourably with his genius in art. Moreover, his offers of the premiums and rewards awaiting the followers of Christ willy-nilly make one think of Tolstoy's intention to write a 'life of Christ as a materialist'—the idea that flashed through his mind during his brother's funeral at Hyères.

VIII

The Millennium

WHEREAS Tolstoy the artist saw life with both eyes wide open, Tolstoy the moralist and the thinker seemed to look at it with one eye only, and even then he brushed aside anything he did not want to see. Whether his conclusions were practicable at all, was not his concern. What mattered was their logical plausibility even if the hidden impulses by which they had been prompted were of the most irrational and fantastic kind. 'I was horrified at my own conclusions and wished not to believe them. And however much these conclusions contradict the whole order of our life, however much they contradict what I previously thought or even expressed, I was obliged to accept them.' This personal statement, taken from his Epilogue to *The Kreutzer Sonata,* holds good for most of his views concerning our moral and social values. Here, too, his old temptation to challenge the 'general tendency' came, of course, into its own. Even on the most important matters Tolstoy used to pass judgment with such unruffled finality as though no one had ever thought about them before. When in moods of this kind, he seemed, moreover, to resist any criticism or suggestion from outside through sheer obstinacy and the spirit of contradiction.

His brother-in-law, C. A. Behrs, during one of his visits, found Tolstoy in bad health and advised him to drink Karlsbad waters. Whereupon the patient declared that no one had ever proved those waters to be of any use, nor could he be persuaded to follow a regular cure. The same witness records another case of this kind. Once, having badly hurt his foot, Tolstoy refused to have a doctor. The pain grew so intense as to make him delirious. At last his wife took matters in her own hands and sent for a surgeon. Tolstoy, who regarded the medical profession as a harmful fraud, received him with scant courtesy, but in the end submitted to him, and soon recovered. In spite of this, his attitude remained unchanged. His bias with regard to doctors was typical of his approach to other and more vital problems. These he tackled with foregone conclusions, prompted to him by his own irrational needs and urges. But for this very reason he insisted all the more on the logical rightness of his doctrines. And since life refused to agree with them, he turned them into a Procrustean bed, calmly chopping off all that did not fit it. This can be said most particularly of his social doctrines.

II

Tolstoy's sociology (or whatever name we give it) was purely subjective and was built up, above all, on his deep-rooted fear of individuation. Refusing to distinguish between individualism and egoism, Tolstoy the moralist was inclined to see in personality something animal and altogether unworthy of human beings whose destiny ought to be universal harmony of the selfless amorphous kind. Such was the voice of his own *daimonion*. His business it was to state this voice in clear logical formulae for the benefit of the world: not as a law of Tolstoy, but of reason itself. In his book, *On Life*, he therefore contends that reason is 'that law to which, for its own happiness, the animal personality of man must be rendered subservient. The animal personality inclines to happiness, reason demonstrates to man the delusion of personal happiness, and leaves but one path. Activity along this path is love. The animal personality of man demands happiness, rational consciousness shows man the misery of all beings who contend with each other, demonstrates to him that there can be no happiness for his animal individual, shows him that the only happiness possible to him is one in which there shall be no contest with other beings, no cessation of happiness, no satiety, in which there shall be no prevision or fear of death.'

Tolstoy actually tried to interpret history itself in terms of progress along the path of de-personalization. The evolution of mankind was divided by him into three periods, corresponding to the three grades of happiness. The first and the lowest degree is the individual or the animal phase (to use Tolstoy's expression) with that selfish kind of happiness which can be won only at the expense of other fellow beings. The second degree is the so-called social phase of human consciousness, in which the individual sacrifices his own well-being to that of some social group or other: the well-being of one's family, clan, State, or nation. The third degree consists, however, of complete selflessness. The individual sacrifices himself to the whole of humanity in which he duly dissolves. The first phase is typical of a savage, the second of a pagan, and the third of a true Christian as Tolstoy wanted him to be.

Self-obliteration for the sake of others thus became the corner-stone for everything Tolstoy taught concerning an ideal society. In *The Kingdom of God Is Within You* he asserted that even the multifarious pagan systems were based on the insignificance of the individual and hence on the idea that true happiness and the meaning of life are to be found only in the undifferentiated group. A man imbued with the Tolstoyan-Christian attitude ought to go, however, much farther. For him life should no longer be centred in his own personality, in his family, or even in his nation, but only in that universal Kingdom of God in which there will be no division of any kind, no separate personalities, no private property, and therefore no friction, no struggle for mine and thine, but only harmony, cemented by 'brotherly love'. Such will in fact be the new epoch which we are now to enter upon, according to Tolstoy. This new attitude has outgrown our previous civic age with its obsolete practices and institutions which, unfortunately, still cling to us. We must adopt a mode of life, corresponding to our present attitude and thus remove the gap between our consciousness and our institutions. It was in the name of such a 'new attitude' that Tolstoy launched his campaign against all the aspects of our social and political life. In this campaign he spared neither friend nor foe. On the other hand, he took it for granted that it was enough to present a clear logical pattern of his views in order to make the world realize how important it was that they should be accepted without delay and without reservation.

Like Socrates, he made no distinction between what is true and what is morally good. The voice of man's conscience (urging us to do good), corroborated by our reason, is, according to him, our only reliable guide. And since its highest dictates are bound to be the same in all men and at all times, they have the same absolute validity as Kant's 'Categorical Imperative'. But if conscience is our only law, what about the other man-made laws which may differ from, or even clash with it? We know that one can often be a criminal before the law, without actually being a sinner before one's own conscience, and vice versa: a conscientious objector, for example. Such a conflict between law and conscience was quite frequent in Russia, where law was only too often a weapon of tyranny in the hands of an unscrupulous minority. But here, too, Tolstoy would contemplate no half-measures. Having sided with conscience, he proclaimed all laws not only superfluous, but even harmful. Organized man-made laws were, in his eyes, the principal guardians of such institutions as State, property, capitalism, militarism—institutions the purpose of which is to foster division and injustice among men. He actually refused to see any difference between law and violence, between functional authority and oppression. So he condemned both, and for moral reasons.

Thus we arrive at the very root of Tolstoy's anarchism which was a result of his moral dictates, allied to his unflinching logic. Both made him turn first of all against all States, all governments, as the organized instruments of violence and division. In his opinion, there was not and could not be such a thing as a good government, since the principle of ruling one's fellow beings was itself utterly bad and immoral. This is what he says about it in *The Kingdom of God Is Within You*: 'Nowadays every government, the despotic as well as the most liberal, has become what Herzen so cleverly termed Genghis Khan with a telegraphic equipment, that is, with an organization of violence, having for its basis nothing less than the most brutal tyranny, and converting all the means invented by science for the intercommunication and peaceful activities of free and equal men, to its own tyrannous and oppressive ends. The existing governments and the ruling classes no longer care to present even the semblance of justice, but rely, thanks to scientific progress, on an organization so ingenious that it is able to enclose all men within a circle of violence through which it is impossible to break.'

This circle of violence was defined by Tolstoy as consisting of four expedients: intimidation, bribery, 'hypnotism', and organized militarism. Through intimidation the State affirms itself as something permanent and immutable in its authority. Through bribery it induces the officials (by means of high salaries) to maintain the system of violence in their own interests. By cleverly devised 'hypnotism' it stupefies people in order to make them cling to outlived forms of existence. And by militarism it defends those outlived forms against internal and external enemies. The circle is complete, as Tolstoy says, and there is no escape.

It all sounds smooth and plausible—at first. But when one looks into the matter thoroughly, one is astonished at the number of other aspects which Tolstoy ignored, and had to ignore, in order to arrive at his own half-truths and simplifications. These are conspicuous also in his condemnation of the organized Christian Church. None of her modern opponents, with the exception of Nietzsche, has used more violent terms in his attacks on her than Tolstoy. Regarding himself as the true interpreter of Christianity, he was obviously intolerant of her interpretations and distortions in which he saw but a continuous betrayal of Christ—in theory and in practice. 'It is not without reason,' he says in the above-mentioned work, 'that all so-called Christian sects believe the Church to be the Scarlet Woman prophesied by the Revelation. It is not without reason that the history of the Church is the history of cruelty and horror.'

III

Tolstoy's rejection of State and Church was only another version of his revolt against the whole of that civilization which cannot be dissociated from the civic and social forms of our life. In *War and Peace* he based his own philosophy of history on the unconscious activities of the masses and argued that any attempt to give these a conscious direction was doomed to be stricken with failure. Now, however, he himself made an attempt consciously to impose upon humanity his own reasoned-out theory of life, the final aim of which was not only to scrap civilization, but to make history itself impossible. All differentiation should be abolished. There should be neither social nor functional difference between one individual and the other. Tolstoy even went so far as to efface the line between manual and mental work in the society to come. Everybody should till the ground with his own hands in order to obtain the food he eats, for in this he saw the law of life. In *What Then Must We Do* he is adamant about the one thing needed—'to fulfil the law of life; to do that which is proper not only to man, but to the animal; to fire off the charge of energy taken in the shape of food, by muscular exertion; to speak in plain language: to earn one's bread. Those who do not work should not eat, or they should earn as much as they have eaten.' He thus only confirms what he had said earlier in his *Confession*: 'A bird is so made that it must fly, collect food, and build a nest, and when I see that a bird does this, I have a pleasure in its joy. A goat, a hare, and a wolf are so made that they must feed themselves, and must breed and feed their family, and when they do so, I feel firmly assured that they are happy and that their life is a reasonable one. Then what should a man do? He, too, should produce his living as the animals do, but with this difference, that he will perish if he does it alone; he must obtain not for himself, but for all. And when he does that, I have a firm assurance that he is happy and that his life is reasonable.'

In his excess of moralizing logic Tolstoy thus came to advocate regression of humanity back to the state of gregarious animals. Not civilization with its inevitable diversity, but amorphous uniformity as near the animal level as possible—such was the core of that Millennium which he eventually offered to mankind. In *The Slavery of our Time* he even went so far as to condemn all technical machines and inventions (including motor-cars, railways, and electric power) on the ground that they can only function by means of that division of labour which perpetuates human inequality and injustice. His foregone conclusion was that 'truly enlightened people will always agree to go back to riding on horses and using pack-horses, or even tilling the earth with sticks and with their own hands rather than travel on railways which regularly every year crush a number of people. The motto for truly enlightened people is not *fiat cultura, pereat justitia,* but *fiat justitia, pereat cultura.*'

Culture (which he never cared to distinguish from sham-culture) was for Tolstoy only another name for injustice, since both were built on inequality and differentiation. But what about the primary natural inequality among men—that of talent, of mental attainments and aspirations—which, in some respects, is even more unjust and puzzling? Tolstoy bypassed this problem, however much he may have insisted, for reasons of his own, on abolishing our social inequality and injustice. But here, too, he went to extremes, and instead of levelling up, he wanted to level down. In *What Then Must We Do* he even denounced habits of cleanliness as a cause of division among men. 'To-day cleanliness consists in changing your shirt once a day, to-morrow in changing it twice a day. To-day the footman's hands must be clean; to-morrow he must wear gloves, and in his clean gloves he must present a letter on a clean salver. And there are no limits to this cleanliness, which is useless to everybody, and objectless, except for the purpose of separating oneself from others, and of rendering impossible all intercourse with them, when this cleanliness is attained by the labour of others. Moreover, when I studied the subject, I came to the conclusion that even what is commonly called education is the very same thing.' After which he jumps to the startling conclusion that 'education consists of those forms and acquirements which are calculated to separate a man from his fellows. And its object is identical with that of cleanliness—to seclude us from the rest of the poor.' Even the most narrow-minded reactionary and opponent of education would probably think it twice over before committing such a strange view to paper.

Dostoevsky once said that whenever Tolstoy the thinker wanted to see an object, he always turned to it his entire body, instead of turning only his head. But this itself was due to his personal need of ignoring those aspects which he did not want to see. He focused his attention only on the vulnerable points of a phenomenon, and exaggerated them to the uttermost, innocently closing his eyes on all the features which were of no use to his argument. His *daimonion* demanded certain conclusions and he got them. Yet we should not forget the fact that Tolstoy simplified or over-simplified from too much complexity. His logic was all the more ruthless the more shaky were the premises with which he had started. But in order to give a final validity to those premises, he was obliged to identify his own inner voice (as well as the moral rules it implied) with that of God Himself. The divine voice or law is higher than any human laws. And in so far as these do not conform to it, they have no right to exist. 'A man needs but to realize that the object of his life is the fulfilment of God's law; then the pre-eminence of that law, claiming as it does his entire allegiance, will of necessity invalidate the authority and restrictions of all human laws,' he says in *The Kingdom of God Is Within You*. 'A Christian who submits to the inner, the divine law, is not only unable to execute the biddings of the outward law when they are at variance with his consciousness of God's law of love, as in the case of the demands made upon him by the government, but he cannot acknowledge the obligation of obeying any individual whomsoever, cannot acknowledge himself to be what is called a subject. . . . The Christian's only guide must be the indwelling element, subject neither to restrictions nor to control.'

IV

Extreme moralism thus touches upon extreme anarchism. But Tolstoy's anarchism is of a passive kind, since it excludes any violence. So much so that, according to Tolstoy, we have no right to resist evil itself in an active manner, that is, by the use of violence. Tolstoy's idea of non-resistance to evil has puzzled a number of minds. But if we accept his initial premise, we must agree that it is logically right. Whether it is intrinsically right is, of course, a different question.

Having deified his own idea of humanity united on the

amorphous pre-individual plane, Tolstoy was logically compelled to reject any act of personal aggression, even should this be in the service of good. Any crime committed upon one's fellow beings is an infringement of the divine law of 'love' in our consciousness. It is an assertion of one's personal self-will against others. But if we resist that crime by violent means, we aggressively assert ourselves, in our turn, against the evil-doer, thereby increasing his own aggressiveness and the already existing division among men. All evil comes from division, but division itself comes from self-assertion. So we have no right to assert ourselves, or our power, even in the defence of a good cause. Such an act would further increase the discord and self-will among men. Evil itself can only be resisted passively.

Quite in keeping with the ruthlessness of his logic, Tolstoy thus advocated (in a letter about Adin Balou's rival theory of non-resistance, 1889) complete passivity even with regard to raving madmen and drunkards. What Tolstoy's sophistications could be like when he wanted to persevere in his fanaticism of logic, is best shown by a letter addressed to E. H. Crosby on the same subject. The problem was whether one ought to kill a robber in order to save a child from being killed by the robber. It was a test case of the theory of non-resistance. But Tolstoy's logic was against the use of any force. Firstly (so he argued), because in such a case the robber himself would be killed, whereas until the very last moment there was no certainty that the robber would actually murder the child. Secondly, to use Tolstoy's own words, there was this irregularity: 'Who has decided that the life of the child is more necessary and better than the life of the robber? But if a man is a Christian, he has still less cause to depart from the law given him by God and to do to the robber what the robber wants to do to the child; he may implore the robber, may place his body between the robber and his victim, but there is one thing he cannot do—he cannot consciously depart from the law of God, the fulfilment of which forms the meaning of life.'

The whole of it sounds like logic run amok through its exaggerated consistency. But apart from this, Tolstoy obviously confused force with violence. It is of course difficult—both ethically and legally—to say where exactly force passes into violence. But this does not mean that the two are identical. The man who uses force in order to save a child from being murdered cannot be accused of violence either on moral or on legal grounds. On the contrary, it would be immoral on his part not to use force in order to prevent such a crime. But Tolstoy wanted to make his logic triumph even against common sense. And common sense tells us that his non-resistance to evil would have only one result in practice: the unscrupulous portion of humanity would take advantage of it and exploit their 'Christian brothers' by the most incredible methods of violence and oppression the world has ever seen.

Tolstoy assures us that whatever happens when violence, State, and civilization are abolished, the 'unknown future' can be no worse than the present. There is no reason why we should fear it, he says. But there is no reason either why we should take his assurances for granted. Nor can we overlook the fact that in his gospel of unity Tolstoy confuses two entirely different phases of human development: the one which precedes individualism, and the other which supersedes it. Even when his reasoning seems to point to the latter (which is rare), his instincts and tendencies remain exclusively on the plane of the outlived pre-individual and pre-civic phase.

Not less disheartening is his alternative to civilization. His aim to reduce all human beings to the same denominator is one of the most unnatural ideals ever devised by man. If it were possible at all, its result would be a vegetative existence outside history and outside any activities which make life worth while. In one of his letters, Tolstoy also gave the following definition of his static Millennium: 'There is but one legitimate life—to receive alms, for Christ's sake, from him who gives, whoever he may be, and to give one's labour to anybody without casting one's accounts, but only feeling one's guilt, constantly wishing to give more than one takes and assuming life to consist in this—this is the only legitimate form of existence.'

This may be existence, but it certainly cannot be called life. And even as existence it would be possible only in some remote Thebaid or in a Buddhist monastery. We have to cope with the complicated tasks, imposed upon us by history and civilization. To betray these by avoiding them means to betray humanity itself. Instead of running away from civilization, along the line of least resistance, we must learn how to overcome and transmute it so as to make it truly creative. We have no right to impoverish our lives even in order to feed the demands of morality—whether private or public. All puritan morality, which tends to narrow down human existence instead of enriching and intensifying it, is immoral for the very reason that it is hostile to life. It can even reach a point where it is logically compelled to insist on the extinction of life. That was the point at which Tolstoy himself eventually arrived. But in order to make this clear we must first say something about Tolstoy's attitude towards sex.

IX

A Puritan's Progress

(Tolstoy and the Sexual Problem)

SEX is that furnace through which, sooner or later, are bound to pass most of our vital problems. It is so closely connected with our moral, social, and spiritual values that individuals and communities can often be judged by their attitude towards it. In strict patriarchal communities, for example, sex is often so little individualized that its only function seems to be the continuation of the race. The need for a mate as a personal complement arises only at a more advanced stage of consciousness: when sexual love itself has become individualized. At this stage self-realization through love and sex can assume an even greater importance than the biological continuity of the race. But at the same time, the dangerous division between love and sex becomes possible. Sex, freed from its exclusive service to the race, can easily degenerate into sensuality and lust, if not checked and guided by the individualized love or Eros. The tension between Sex and Eros can in fact grow to such an extent as to fluctuate between the ideal of pure womanhood and the promiscuous female; between Dante's seraphic love for Beatrice and the perversities of decaying civilizations. A certain split between Sex and Eros occurs, at some time or other, in every individual. And unless he overcomes it by means of an integrating process, the conflict will increase or else lead to one-sided evasions which will only complicate the issue. One of such evasions is the indulgence of sex for its own sake. But its opposite, the ascetic or puritan negation of sex, is equally one-sided. Most painful of all is, however, that alternation of the two which, for a long time, was typical also of Leo Tolstoy.

Even Tolstoy's early works and diaries testify to this split between sex and love. Such of his stories as *Youth, A Landowner's Morning,* and especially *Family Happiness,* afford us many a glimpse of his nostalgia for a pure woman. In the second half of *Family Happiness* the heroine is even turned, significantly enough, into a desexualized mother. Yet, according to his own diaries, Tolstoy in those very years indulged in sexual excesses which formed the greatest possible contrast to his dreams. The truth being that his sexuality was often stronger than either his dreams of purity or even his moral disapproval. In the end, it became an obsession with him which he could fight only by means of self-imposed moral rules on the one hand, and by hostility towards women on the other. Even in his old age he fully retained his rancour with regard to women, and its causes were perhaps deeper than moral self-protection. 'He talks most of God, of peasants, and of women,' Gorky says in his reminiscences of the aged Tolstoy. 'Woman in my opinion he regards with implacable hostility and loves to punish her. . . . It is hostility of the male who has not succeeded in getting all the pleasure he could, or it is the hostility of spirit against the degrading impulses of flesh. But it is hostility, and cold, as in *Anna Karenina.*'

The secret of it goes back to the split between love and sex in him—a split which in his early years was partly fostered by his unattractive exterior and by the shyness resulting from it. 'I was too egotistical', he says in *Youth,* 'to become accustomed to my position, and consoled myself, like the fox, by assuring myself that the grapes were still green; that is to say, I endeavoured to despise all the pleasures derived from a pleasing exterior, and I strained every nerve of my mind and imagination to find solace in proud solitude.' Too shy to aspire to the pleasures of true love, he either denied its existence or else tried to give his nostalgia a vague humanitarian direction. In the same work he classified love into three categories: beautiful love, self-sacrificing love, active love, with the significant remark: 'I do not speak of the love of a young man for a young girl, and hers for him. I fear these tendernesses, and have been so unfortunate in life as never to have seen a single spark of truth in this species of love, but only a lie, in which sentiment, connubial relations, money, a desire to bind and to unbind one's hands, have to such an extent confused the feeling itself, that it has been impossible to disentangle it. I am speaking of the love for man, which, according to the greater or lesser power of the soul, concentrates itself upon one, upon several, or pours itself upon many: of the love of mother, father, brother, children, for a comrade, friends, fellow countrymen, in short of love for humanity.'

Even here his love for humanity (which later merged with what he called Christian love) sounds like a substitute for his unsatisfied sexual love. The question is whether, in his case, a reconciliation between sex and love was possible at all, since the split between them was much too deep. And one of the reasons for the split itself may have been the loss of his mother before he was two years old. The image of the mother remained an object of his conscious and unconscious longing. And the purity of that image made the very thought of sexual relations look not only as a moral fall, but as a sacrilege. How potent that sentimental and infantile longing really was can be gathered from the already quoted lines, which he wrote in his diary at the age of seventy-two. 'Dull, miserable state the whole day. Towards the evening this mood passed into tenderness—a desire for fondness, for love; I longed as children do to press up to a loving, pitying human being, to weep with emotion and to be comforted. But whom could I come close to like this? I think of all the people I loved, and not one of them can offer me the sympathy I need. If I only could become little again and snuggle up to my mother as I imagine her to myself! Yes, yes, mother whom I called to when I could not speak; she—my highest image of pure love; not cold, divine love, but earthly, warm, motherly. It is that for which my battered, weary soul is longing.'

It is not too much to say that Tolstoy's call for his equalizing Christian love sprang in essence from the same need: the need for an all-embracing protecting Mother whose love makes no distinction between one child and another. Such an image may be connected with the symbol of the Madonna and of that pure love which is the negation of sex. On the other hand, Tolstoy was also a being made of flesh and blood, even something of an impetuous 'troglodyte' (to use Turgenev's expression), whose sex demanded satisfaction no matter what his morals said to it. And since he could do so only by insulting his 'image of pure love', any gratification of sexual desire was afterwards felt by him as a sin or a crime which had to be expiated. Hence the invariable remorse and suffering after each 'fall'. In fact, the more he fell a prey to temptations of his flesh, the greater was his moral aftermath with all its self-accusations, 'rules', and attacks on women. These two entries, taken from his diary, are typical. The first, dating from his undergraduate years in Kazan (1846–7), reads: 'I will set myself yet another rule—as follows. Regard feminine society as an inevitable evil of social life, and in so far as you can, avoid it. From whom, indeed, do we learn voluptuousness, effeminacy, frivolity in everything, and many another vice, if not from women? Who is responsible for the fact that we lose such feelings inherent in us as courage, fortitude, prudence, equity, and so forth, if not woman?' A few years later (1852) he made an even more sweeping generalization: 'Love does not exist. There exists the physical need for intercourse, and the rational need for a mate in life.'

The cleavage between love and sex remained so wide in him that even while writing his puritanic novel, *Family Happiness,* he indulged in fits of carnal lust. In 1858, that is, some four years before his marriage, he moreover contracted a liaison with a peasant woman. Her name was Aksinya and she was the wife of one of his own serfs. Judging by Tolstoy's diaries, she must have appealed to all that was primitive and elementally passionate in him. Besides, she belonged to those very masses which were so near, organically near, to Tolstoy. 'I simply tremble with fear when I think how akin she is to me,' he wrote on May 12th, 1860. And a fortnight later, he made this startling confession: 'I no longer feel like a stag with regard to her, but as though I were her husband. Strangely enough, I wish I could arouse in me my former satiety, but cannot.'

Aksinya attracted him above all as 'Nature herself': as a healthy full-blooded animal, capable of satisfying the satyr, the troglodyte, in him. But his moral double, constantly watching and censoring, would not approve of it. Hence the revolt against sex in *Family Happiness.* Hence *The Devil* with its formidable analysis of the split between love and sex. As a matter of fact, the story itself refers to Tolstoy's infatuation with Aksinya shortly before he had fallen in love with the pretty Sophia Andreyevna Behrs, whom he married in 1862.

II

The happy married life of Kitty and Levin, as shown in *Anna Karenina,* is a somewhat idealized transformation of Tolstoy's own experience. For if we consult his and also his wife's diaries, referring to that period, we find a less idyllic picture. On August 23rd, 1862 Tolstoy made this entry: 'I stayed overnight with the Behrses. She is a child. So it seems. The whole of it is a mess. If only one could see things clearly and honestly. I am afraid of myself: what am I to do if this also is only a wish to love and not love itself?' Yet less than a month later he seemed to have shed all the doubts. 'I never thought I could be so much in love,' he wrote on September 12th. 'I am mad and will shoot myself if things go on like this. Spent the evening in their house. She is charming in every respect.' A couple of weeks later she was his wife.

Married life with a beautiful woman whom he loved should have opened up for him the prospect of a more harmonious and integrated inner life. But nothing of the sort happened, and partly through his wife's fault. Sexually not yet properly awakened and still too much of a child (she was only eighteen), Sophia Andreyevna could hardly understand her husband's inner dilemma. Nonplussed, perhaps even frightened by his passion, she was unable to handle the 'stag' in Tolstoy in the right way. Besides, she was too much of a mother by nature to pay much attention to sex for which she seemed to have developed a kind of physical loathing. In a parable written at the time, Tolstoy referred to his undersexed wife as a 'porcelain puppet'. And since a puppet was unable to integrate his sex and his love, his carnal desire remained as impetuous as ever and—judging by his wife's diaries—at times almost brutal.

No wonder that the memory of Aksinya kept on haunting him. To make things worse, Tolstoy was unable to bury his 'vicious' past and let it take care of itself. In a fit of moral self-righteousness, he had shown to his inexperienced bride the diary of his bachelor days. The impression made upon her can be imagined. This is what she wrote in her own diary on October 8th, 1862: 'When I got married, I had to admit that my old dreams were foolish, and yet I feel unable to give them up altogether. The *whole* of my husband's past is so dreadful that I don't think I shall ever be able to accept it. Unless, of course, I acquire some new interest in life, such as children, whom I want terribly, for they alone will give me a sound future and will enable me to see things in a pure light, without his past, without all the filth I still see in him, and which makes me so unhappy. . . . He likes to torture me and to see me weep, because he has no faith in me. It instinctively annoys him that I should have gained happiness so easily, without reflection, without previous suffering. Gradually I shall retreat into myself and shall poison his life. . . . Surely, it does not make him happy to see me weep and to make me realize that there is something wrong in our relations, and that sooner or later, we will drift apart in the spiritual sense. . . .' And three days later: 'I am terribly sad and take refuge in myself. My husband is ill, bad-tempered, and doesn't love me. I expected it and yet didn't know it would be so dreadful. I wonder where people get the idea of my immense happiness.'

Sophia Andreyevna was even compelled to put up with the occasional vicinity of her husband's former mistress Aksinya, the truth about whom she had learned from her husband's diaries. Living in the same village and working now and then in or near Tolstoy's house, Aksinya could not avoid being seen by the young Countess whose reactions to such meetings can be imagined. 'Some day I shall kill myself with jealousy,' she wrote in her diary on December 6th, 1862. ' "Never so much in love as now!" ' [1] And nothing but a big fat lump of a woman. Terrible! I kept looking at his daggers and rifles with the greatest joy. One jerk—it's so easy. So long as there is no child. And there she is, a few yards from here. It drives me mad! I shall go out for a drive. I may meet her at any moment. So that's how he loved her! If only I could burn his diary and his whole past!'

Tolstoy's inner cleavage remained the same also in his marriage. Hence his irritation and resentment against his wife who could not even grasp what the matter was. Nor was she able to give the same satisfaction to her husband's unsublimated sex which Aksinya, 'that big fat lump of a woman',

[1] Referring to a sentence in Tolstoy's diary.

had once afforded him. Misunderstandings between husband and wife thus became inevitable and were bound to grow. 'Lyova[1] is breaking away from me,' she wrote on April 29th, 1863. 'The physical side of love matters a great deal to him. That's dreadful—for it is exactly the other way round with me.' In her entry on May 8th of the same year she was even more outspoken as a wife: 'I feel I am distasteful to him. . . . I can bring him no joy of any kind as long as I am pregnant. How sad that a wife can only learn during her pregnancy whether or not her husband really loves her.'

Naïve as she was, Sophia Andreyevna hardly ever suspected the real cause of Tolstoy's irritation which, in his case, amounted to a tragedy. He knew, of course, periods of relative contentment, but the polarity between asceticism on the one hand, and carnal lust on the other, remained as strong in him as before. In the end he looked upon sexual relations even with his own wife as a 'fall', yet he could not give them up. The self-accusation which he jotted down in his diary on October 22, 1879, that is, seventeen years after his marriage, shows clearly what he felt like. 'There are people with big mighty wings who, because of their sensuality lower themselves to the level of the crowd where they break their wings. Such am I. There one's wings beat, soar up, and down one falls again. If my wings get well again, I will soar into great heights. So help me God!' But it was all in vain—as long as his sex remained alive and virile. No wonder that even in his old age Tolstoy complained to Gorky that the greatest of all tragedies is the tragedy of the connubial bed.

Meanwhile, Sophia Andreyevna—an ideal mother and a loyal wife if ever there was one—was too much *terre-à-terre* to understand her husband's dilemma. She attributed it all to his irritable temper, his restlessness, and his incurable sensuality. How much she was inclined to simplify him (especially in her rancorous moods) is proved by this verdict, en-

[1] Lyova and Lyovochka are diminutives of Leo (Lyov in Russian).

tered in her diary on November 20th, 1890—more than ten years after Tolstoy's conversion: 'I see now clearly that I idealized him, without realizing that there was nothing in him except sensuality.' And as though in confirmation of this, she inserted on December 17th: 'All the harshness and difference has melted away and has resolved itself in the usual thing.' We must remember that when this particular 'usual thing' happened, Tolstoy was sixty-two and had already started his savage onslaught on sexual relations not only without but even within married life. And twenty years later, on August 20th, 1910, Sophia Andreyevna had enough common sense (but only common sense) to condemn her husband's exaggerated asceticism as follows: 'That would be all very well if Leo Nikolayevitch were a monk, an ascetic, and lived a celibate life. But at his wish I have been pregnant sixteen times: thirteen children born and three miscarriages. In those days he suggested to me, a young woman, that he could not work or write well if I refused to cohabit with him.'

III

It is surprising that, in spite of this, Tolstoy the artist revealed to the world some of the most wonderful aspects of true passion and of true love which he fully justified from the standpoint of life. Unfortunately, after his conversion Tolstoy the puritan wanted to justify life itself from the standpoint of his own moral rules. Even in *War and Peace* and especially in *Anna Karenina,* his lovers fall into two categories. Pierre and Natasha, Nicholas Rostov and Princess Mary, Levin and Kitty, are all in the category of virtue, and earn due rewards. The adulteress Anna and her lover Vronsky, who are on the side of passion and sin, must, however, be punished. And Tolstoy the puritan punished both of them so severely that the denouement of *Anna Karenina* leads up to *The Kreutzer Sonata* on the one hand, and to *Resurrection* on the other.

The Kreutzer Sonata is not on the level of Tolstoy's best literary achievements. Deliberately bald and rugged, it keeps only to the essentials, and so outspokenly, too, as to stun the reader. Poznyshov, the hero of this narrative, has murdered in a fit of jealousy his own wife. On his acquittal, he relates (in a railway carriage) the motive and the details of his crime. But the story itself is used by Tolstoy as a pretext for piling up indictments against sex, women, marriage, culture—against anything in fact which spells danger to Tolstoy's own ideal of society and virtue. And Poznyshov's language is fully in keeping with the theme. This is how he defines love between the two sexes: 'Women are well aware that what is commonly called sublime and poetical love, depends not on moral qualities, but on frequent meetings, and on the style in which the hair is done up, and on the colour and cut of the dress. . . . Every coquette is keenly conscious of this; every innocent girl is unconsciously aware of this. Hence these odious jerseys and projections behind, these exposed shoulders, arms, and almost open breasts. Women, particularly those who have passed through the masculine school, are alive to the fact that conversations on lofty themes are mere hollow phrases, that the object of a man's desire is the person, and whatever sets that out in its most seductive light; and they act in strict accordance with this knowledge.'

After thirty years of married life, Tolstoy thus reiterated—through his mouthpiece Poznyshov—the same views about love and sex which he had once expressed as a youth of twenty-four: that there is no love, but only the physical need for intercourse and the rational need for a mate in life. But this time he was much more intolerant with regard to both. 'What is particularly revolting about all this, is that whereas in theory love is described as an ideal state, a sublime sentiment, in practice it is a thing which cannot be mentioned without a feeling of disgust. It was not without cause that nature made it so. But if it is revolting, let it be proclaimed so without any disguise. Instead of that, however, people go about preaching and teaching that it is something splendid and sublime.'

Woman, the notorious tool of the devil, receives her due in full. We see how an ascetic on principle defies sex and women precisely because he is afraid of them, afraid even of the thought of them. In his opinion, 'woman has transformed herself into an object of pleasure of such terrible effect that a man cannot calmly approach her. No sooner does a man draw near a woman than he falls under the power of her spell. Even in former times I always felt ill at ease in the presence of a lady arrayed in all the splendour of ball-dresses; at present I positively shudder at the sight, for I recognize therein a palpable danger to people in general, a danger that has no legal right to exist; and I feel prompted to call a policeman, to appeal for protection against this danger that threatens me, or to insist on its removal or suppression.'

Poor morality which wants temptations to be removed by the police for fear of succumbing to them. But such is the general tenor of *The Kreutzer Sonata* with its wild attacks and intolerance. Tolstoy himself suspected what was behind it, for in the spring 1891 he wrote to a friend: 'There must have been something bad in my *Kreutzer Sonata.* I am utterly fed up with it, with every reminiscence of it. There was something nasty in the motives which dominated me, while I wrote it. . . . I will try to avoid it in future, provided I happen to write something or other.' [1]

This passage should perhaps be completed by a few lines

[1] As many people considered *The Kreutzer Sonata* almost a disguised reflection of Tolstoy's attitude towards his own wife, Sophia Andreyevna wrote, in answer, a variation of her own (which never appeared in print). In that story the wife—an innocent ethereal beauty—is married to a sensual animal. A consumptive artist falls platonically in love with her, but her husband is too thick-skinned to understand such idealistic relations and kills her in a fit of jealousy. Also one of Tolstoy's sons (Leo) wrote a story, *Chopin's Prelude,* which is a complete negation of the standpoint represented by *The Kreutzer Sonata.*

from one of Tolstoy's letters to his friend, the painter N. N. Gay. It concerns one of those colonies the members of which lived according to Tolstoy's moral principles and practised complete sexual abstinence even in marriage—quite in the spirit of the Epilogue to *The Kreutzer Sonata*. 'A—n came to see me in the autumn,' wrote Tolstoy, 'he and all of them live wonderfully. The sexual problem, for example, they have solved by complete abstinence, a holy life. But—may Lord forgive my sins—my impression was a heavy one. Not that out of my sloth I envy their life; on the contrary, I see their moral height and rejoice in it as though it were my own; yet something is wrong in all that. Do not show this letter, my dear; it might grieve them.'

In spite of such flashes of insight, Tolstoy continued to preach, if not to practise, the same abstinence with unflagging zeal. His last big novel, *Resurrection,* contains attacks on sex which surpass even those in *The Kreutzer Sonata*. Nekhlyudov's 'Christian love' for the prostitute and supposed murderess Katyusha Maslova is of course utterly sexless. But for this very reason it is also forced, insincere, and tainted with that selfish pity which makes Tolstoy himself wince at times. What mattered to Nekhlyudov was not Maslova, but the peace of his own conscience. He was concerned with his own 'salvation' and not with hers. Yet Tolstoy the puritan welcomed even this kind of 'love' as a blow to sex. The blow itself was accompanied by a frontal attack of the most vicious kind. As it happened, Maslova was befriended by the pretty political exile Marya Pavlovna—a girl so selfless that the 'interest of her whole life lay in searching for opportunities to serve others just as the sportsman searches for game'. And this educated girl who had renounced her home, wealth, and freedom in order to serve others, soon discovered a common ground on which she was able to meet that ex-prostitute as a companion, even as a friend. In Tolstoy's own words, 'they were united by the repulsion they both felt for sexual love.

The one loathed that love, having experienced all its horrors; the other, never having experienced it, looked at it as something repugnant and offensive to human dignity.'

Is, then, love nothing more than what a criminal prostitute knows about it? And is it not unpardonable on the part of the aged Tolstoy that in his puritanic zeal to lower woman, he did all in his power to debase sexual love, too, to mere mud? But having failed to integrate love and sex, he was bound to think of the two in terms of antitheses—one excluding the other. The gap between them grew wider and wider. Finally sex in general was proclaimed by him dirt and abomination, whereas desexualized love was raised on to the pedestal of philanthropy, goodness, and abstract 'universal brotherhood' as Tolstoy understood it. Another political prisoner, Simonson, to whom we are introduced in *Resurrection,* had formulated (during his previous exile) a religious teaching which governed all his activities. And the highest aim of that teaching was celibacy. In full agreement with the converted Tolstoy he 'thought that procreation was a lower function of man, the higher function being to serve already existing lives. He found support for this theory in the fact that there exist phagocytes in the blood. Celibates, according to his opinion, were like phagocytes, whose mission it is to help the weak and sick parts of the organism. From the moment he came to this conclusion, he lived accordingly, though in his youth he had been dissipated; and he considered himself, and Marya Pavlovna as well, to be human phagocytes.'

IV

For further deductions we must go back to *The Kreutzer Sonata* and its *Epilogue*. Unable to accept and ennoble sex, Tolstoy was compelled to fight it with a virulence equal only to his fear of it. This fear gradually drove him to increasingly desperate measures of self-protection, until he began to advocate complete abolition of sex in the name of morality and virtue. But if you abolish sex, you destroy the human race itself the existence of which depends on sexual intercourse. Tolstoy the puritan not only was not afraid of such a conclusion, but even welcomed it with enthusiasm in *The Kreutzer Sonata.*

According to his wife's testimony, Tolstoy's own 'passion of the senses', was particularly riotous at the period of his writing that story. But this, in its turn, may only have increased the ruthlessness with which he wanted to abolish sex even at the risk of a universal suicide. In fact, he now combined his ideal of a universal beehive unity with a gospel of universal suicide. 'If the object for which humanity strives is bliss, goodness, love or by whatever other name you like to call it; if it is what the ancient prophets have proclaimed it to be, namely that all men be united in love, that their swords be turned into ploughshares, and so on, what hinders the accomplishment of this object? The passions do. Now, of all the passions, the strongest, the most wicked, the most stubborn is the passion of the senses. Consequently, if we succeed in rooting up the passions and with them this last and most powerful, the prophecies will come to pass; men will be united by the bond of love, the aim and mission of humanity will have been fulfilled, and there will no longer be any reason for the further existence of the human race. . . . The human race will cease? Yes; but is it possible that any one, no matter from what point of view he contemplated the world, could have even entertained a doubt about that? Why, it is inevitable as death. All ecclesiastical doctrines are based on the theory that this world of ours will sooner or later come to an end; modern science propagates the same teaching. Why should we be surprised that ethics inculcate the same lesson?'

The idea could hardly be expressed more clearly. Tolstoy's puritanism thus blended with his gospel of the amorphous humanity, and the result was—a call to nothingness, the apotheosis of Nirvana. But in his case such a course was to be expected, not only logically, but also psychologically. Unintegrated sex means unintegrated personality, which thus cannot develop according to its own creative laws. So it is bound to turn, sooner or later, against itself, against sex, against the whole of life. A puritan who loathes sex, because he has failed to sublimate it, often cannot help identifying sexual intercourse with moral pollution. And since the procreation of mankind is possible only at the price of such pollution, then the very existence of mankind appears to him as something immoral. The end of the human race may, therefore, become not only desirable but even morally imperative. Among Tolstoy's thoughts about the relation of the sexes (collected by V. Chertkov) we read these incredible lines: 'What is it that so revolts men in the idea that moral righteous life will also bring the race to an end? Perhaps the one and the other will coincide. In a Shaker article this is even suggested. It is stated there, "Why should not men by abstinence deliver themselves from violent death?" Excellent.'

This is how radical puritanism can pass into nihilism, into the negation of mankind—all in the name of morality or even brotherly love. But who wishes to destroy what he loves? In his diary, on August 1st, 1896, Tolstoy actually says, that 'to love an individual one must be blinded. Without being blinded one can love only God, but people can be pitied, which means, loved in a godly way.' His own 'godly love' for mankind often reminds one of Nekhlyudov's love for the prostitute Maslova in *Resurrection*. It is a puritan's love, full of principles, but devoid of true warmth and generosity. There was, moreover, hidden rancour underneath it all. This rancour came out in the later stages of his conjugal life, and even in his amazing flight from family and home.

X

The Last Act

THERE are still a number of conjectures about Tolstoy's sensational flight from his family in October 1910—a flight during which he died at the age of eighty-two. Was such a step a spiritual feat, or was it merely an act of despair on the part of a man who wanted to have peace, at last, not only from his disciples and worshippers, but also from his family, and especially from his wife? Most likely it was a combination of several motives, even if there can no longer be any doubt that misunderstandings with his wife must have played the principal part in the drama.

The long years of Tolstoy's married life, far from alleviating, only increased the inner differences between him and Sophia Andreyevna. Essentially a mother and a *Hausfrau,* with a bourgeois sense of values, she always regarded her family duties, the care for her children and the management of the house, as more real and more important than her husband's gropings for abstract truths, however much she appreciated his artistic genius. Tolstoy, on the other hand, had begun to sense an additional danger in this even during the first year of his marriage. As far back as June 2nd, 1863, he jotted in his diary: 'It is terrible and stupid to pin one's happiness to material conditions—wife, children, health, riches. . . . I feel small and despicable. And I became so after having married the woman I love.'

As though attempting a temporary postponement of his vital problems, the married Tolstoy concentrated his energies not only on artistic creations, but for a while also on those material activities which were so dear to his *terre-à-terre* wife. The instinct of a patriarchal landowner was sufficiently strong in him to make him increase his prosperity and even to idealize the matronly qualities of his own wife (in the married Natasha and even more in the married Kitty). But this did not last long. The family and its prosperity was perhaps the only ground on which Tolstoy and his wife could meet without friction and where they enjoyed even periods of happiness. For this very reason Tolstoy's conversion came as a shock to Sophia Andreyevna. Not only was she indifferent to her husband's new 'religion', but turned intensely hostile when Tolstoy wanted to try it on his own family. In this manner a new conflict was added to the already existing differences between him and her. And she was as obstinate as was he. 'With nine children I could not, like a weather-cock, turn in the ever-changing direction of my husband's spiritual going away,' she defends herself in her autobiography. 'With him it was a passionate, sincere seeking; with me it would have been a silly imitation, positively harmful to the family. . . . If I had given away all my fortune at my husband's desire (I don't know to whom); if I had been left in poverty with nine children on hand, I would have had to work for the family—to feed, to do sewing for, wash, bring up my children without education. Leo Nikolayevitch, by vocation and inclination, could have done nothing else but write.'

Unwilling to serve, together with her children, as an illustration of her husband's doctrines, Sophia Andreyevna bravely shouldered the management of the estate and of the entire family. Meanwhile, Tolstoy not only kept on denouncing private property as evil, but in 1884 gave up this evil altogether, as far as he himself was concerned: he shifted it upon his wife. True enough, he continued to live in comfort on his estate, wondering why, with all his belief in persuasion, he was yet unable to make his wife follow him in matters which he considered so important an inspiration from on high. Was there anything wrong with his teaching? He himself complained that 'the disagreement of people is exceedingly painful, especially when man thinks of himself that he has not his own opinions, but only holds the truth. Then suddenly it turns out that the truth not only is not understood, but that it actually offends people and drives them away. There is something wrong here, I am to blame for something, I have in a way offended the truth itself. This is terrible, and it torments me.' All the same Sophia Andreyevna persisted in her own truth. And she knew why.

II

Tolstoy could not help resenting such a disagreement on the part of his wife. He was inclined to see in it petty motives, stupidity, and even malice. The situation became aggravated by periodic quarrels, the virulence and cruelty of which were on the increase. The only logical step would have been divorce. Judging by a letter written by Sophia Andreyevna to her sister Tanya in 1885, Tolstoy had actually threatened to divorce his wife, and on one occasion had even shouted at her: 'Wherever you are the very air becomes poisoned.' This is what he himself wrote in his diary on October 2nd, 1886: 'To get away, one way or another, from this house or from this life, to leave all this cruelty, these impossible demands—such is the thought that keeps on haunting me day and night.' What his own cruelty could be like is best shown by the following episode, told by Aylmer Maude in his biography of Tolstoy. After several misunderstandings, Tolstoy left his wife in 1887, on the very evening when she gave birth to her youngest daughter Alexandra. The birth pangs were long and unusually painful. Yet the Countess refused to go to her room and sat in the garden, weeping. Fortunately, the vanished Tolstoy had thought it over and returned at five o'clock in the morning. The Countess went to him in his study, but he was so preoccupied with the 'struggle in his own soul' that he had no words of solace or kindness for her. . . . Their relations only deteriorated as years passed. It is strange to read this accusation in Sophia Andreyevna's diary (September 22nd, 1897) at the time when Tolstoy was ardently preaching the gospel of Christian love and kindness: 'If only the world knew how little of tender sincere kindness there is in him, and how many actions of his come from his principles and not from the kindness of his heart.'

What made things worse was the fact that even in his old age Tolstoy's suppressed 'passion of the senses' had its outbursts which his undersexed wife had to satisfy. As she complains in her diaries, his sexual appetite was particularly strong during his *Kreutzer Sonata* period, that is, when he denied the same appetite to everybody else. Nor could she help seeing with what gusto the hidden Epicurean in Tolstoy enjoyed some of those very amenities and benefits of civilization which he regarded as immoral and even criminal. And as for Tolstoy's self-accusations, she probably smiled at them, as she smiled at some of his other weaknesses. Yet wounded by her husband's treatment, she gradually began to magnify them, as if taking revenge upon him. It must have been in one of such moods that she wrote on September 22nd, 1897: 'I do not believe in his goodness and love of humanity. I know the only source of his action: glory and more glory, insatiable, boundless, feverish.' On August 27th, 1910, that is, in the period immediately preceding Tolstoy's flight, she complained that her daughter Tanya had fifty-eight photographs of him 'taken at every possible angle and in all positions, at every possible place and with a variety of smiles and grimaces.' And two months later (October 20th): 'How eagerly and ardently Leo Nikolayevitch reads all that is written and printed about him in the papers! Evidently he can never give that up!'

A one-sided view can often be much more misleading than

a downright lie. When irritated—and this was a frequent disposition with her during the last years of Tolstoy's life—Sophia Andreyevna was often incapable of seeing her husband in his true perspective: with all his weaknesses and virtues, and without exaggerating some at the expense of others. What made this tragedy of errors even more painful was her delusion that her husband's coldness towards her was caused not by her lack of understanding, but by the fact that she knew him much too well. She apparently thought that Tolstoy resented her perspicacity by virtue of which he could not appear a superman and a hero in the eyes of his own wife. This passage from her diary (December 1890) gives her away, and hardly to her advantage: 'It occurs to me that you can't really love some one who knows you intimately, with all your weaknesses and to whom you can't show only one side of the medal.'

The duel between these two aged people, who had been married for nearly half a century, is a painful sight. The more so because in relations with his own wife Tolstoy himself often lacked that clairvoyance and human understanding which he showed with regard to his fictitious characters. As a young bridegroom he wrote after his wedding in 1862 that his happiness was too unspeakable to last. As a man of seventy-two he had a different tale to tell. Thus, on July 16th, 1901, he noted down: 'Only husbands get to know women (when it is too late). Only husbands see what they are like behind the scenes.' And nine years later, on the forty-eighth anniversary of his wedding: 'To-day, remembering my wedding, I thought that it was just a fatality. I was never even in love. But I could not avoid marrying.'

These avowals went hand-in-hand with his deliberate disparagement of women, his own wife included. His bitterness towards her was increased by his reluctance to go away from his home (so competently run by her) and thus live up to his own convictions. 'Woman is the tool of the devil,' he thunders in his diary on August 3rd, 1898. 'She is generally stupid, but the devil lends her his brains when she works for him. Here you see, she has done miracles of thinking, farsightedness, constancy, in order to do something nasty; but as soon as something not nasty is needed, she cannot understand the simplest thing; she cannot see farther than the present moment, and there is no self-control and no patience.' On November 20th of the same year he stated even more explicitly: 'For seventy years I have been lowering and lowering my opinion of women and still it has to be lowered more and more.' In the same year he said to the pianist Goldenveizer: 'I tell you in secret and you must not talk about it: woman is generally so bad that the difference between a good and a bad woman scarcely exists. . . . One day, I will write about women. When I am quite old, and my indigestion is completely out of order, I will pop my head out and tell them: "This is what you are like!" and then disappear completely, otherwise they would peck me to death.'

Such was Tolstoy's final conclusion in which, no doubt, the misunderstandings with his wife had their share. Sophia Andreyevna's position was the more difficult as in her own possessive way she really loved her husband, and was morbidly jealous of his attachments and affections. The aged Tolstoy, on the other hand, now looked upon her mainly as a brake on the path of his moral self-perfection, or—to quote his own words—as a mill-stone round his neck. Nor did Tolstoy show any particular interest in his grown-up children, with the exception of his youngest daughter Alexandra, who was his follower. But the 'worldly' care for them was no longer his concern. All that was now in his wife's hands whom he, nevertheless, continued to reproach and to torment, often without any justification. In one of her entries Sophia Andreyevna remarked, with bitter irony, that if the salvation of man's soul consisted in worrying the life out of a near one, then her husband was sure to be among the saved. Little wonder that in the end she became a nervous wreck, suffering from hysteria and at times even from a loss of mental balance.

III

It was in those years that Yasnaya Polyana had to put up with the intrusion of a new element: the worshipping Tolstoyans. They kept on flocking to Tolstoy's residence, and their enthusiasm for the bliss conferred upon them by his teaching stood in sharp contrast to the scepticism of Sophia Andreyevna. Tolstoy often had to pretend to be as naïve as his followers. In order not to disappoint their expectations he even had to 'live for show', as he once said to Gorky. But on the other hand, he found in their enthusiasm a moral support—a safeguard against his own hidden scepticism which was of a much more sinister brand than that of his wife.

Sophia Andreyevna did her best to play the part of a good hostess, although her opinion of the Tolstoyans was, to put it mildly, not very flattering. 'What disagreeable characters all these disciples of Leo Nikolayevitch are! Not a single sane person among them,' she wrote in March, 1887. In another passage she refers to the whole collection as 'miserable abortions of human society, aimless babblers, uneducated loafers'. But there were also ambitious and crafty men among them, one of whom, Vladimir Chertkov, soon played a fatal role in Tolstoy's household.

Formerly a dashing officer in the guards, Chertkov embraced Tolstoy's doctrine with fanatical zest. He, moreover, soon discovered certain weak spots in his teacher's character and began to exploit them for the advancement of his own plans. Cold and calculating, with the mentality of a sectarian, he was endowed not only with a strong will, but also with organizing power, energy, and with a boundless capacity for both flattery and intrigue. It is significant that his appearance in Tolstoy's household at once aroused distrust in Sophia Andreyevna. 'I do not like him: he is clever and sly and one-sided, and is not a good man,' she jotted down on March 6th, 1887. 'Leo Nikolayevitch is very partial to him.' She was more outspoken in her entry three days later. 'That blunt, sly, untruthful man, having succeeded in getting round Leo Nikolayevitch with his flattery, is now trying (I suppose that's Christian) to destroy the bond which has so closely kept us together for nearly twenty years.'

She was right. Tolstoy the teacher received from Chertkov that unswerving adulation which he had perhaps expected, but in vain, from his own wife. He and Chertkov soon became inseparable. Chertkov, with his despotic ways, set out to gain complete mastery over Tolstoy. But in order to do this, he first had to crush Sophia Andreyevna's opposition. He found a short cut in deliberately fostering the tension between Tolstoy and his wife, and in the end he triumphed. It was also he who, amongst other things, blamed Sophia Andreyevna for Tolstoy's failure to live up to his own teaching in practice. She, on the other hand, only became more nervous and bewildered. In her morbid imagination she interpreted Tolstoy's friendship for Chertkov even as a kind of senile erotic attachment. Things went so far that in the end the very presence of Chertkov in her house was enough to give her fits of hysteria.

Matters came to a head in the summer of 1910. Under some pretext or other, Chertkov succeeded in obtaining from Tolstoy those of his diaries which he had kept secret even from his own wife. Apprehensive about the possible bad references to herself, Sophia Andreyevna insisted that the diaries should be returned. Chertkov refused, while Tolstoy himself seemed both helpless and will-less. The atmospheres of wrangles, of mutual suspicion, of slander and spying reached at times fantastic proportions. The level to which it had sunk can be judged by Sophia Andreyevna's entry, dated July 1st, 1910: 'Chertkov has been rude to me. I demanded that he should return Leo Nikolayevitch's diaries for the last ten years which he has been keeping, and which Leo Nikolayevitch has forgotten. He said to me: "Are you afraid I shall show you up by means of the diaries? I have had it in my power for a long time, and I have sufficient influence to smirch you and your family and if I have not done so it is only out of affection for Leo Nikolayevitch." And then he added: "Had I such a wife, I should long ago have shot myself or run to America." '

And Tolstoy, instead of shielding his wife from Chertkov, seemed to shield Chertkov from her. Hysterical scenes and remonstrations finally became too much for him. Once again he began to think of going away. What he wanted was peace, and peace was out of the question as long as he stayed at home. 'Last night Sonya was weak and irritable,' he wrote on July 1st, 1909. 'I woke up feeling weak. I went to see her. It was something insane. . . . I am tired and cannot stand it and feel quite ill. I feel I cannot be loving and reasonable, absolutely cannot. At present I only want to keep away and take no part. There is nothing else I can do, or else I have seriously thought of escaping. Now then, show your Christianity. *C'est le moment ou jamais.* But I awfully want to go away. I doubt if my presence here is of use to anyone. Help me, O Lord, teach me. There is only one thing I want to do —not my will, but Thine.'

The Lord did not seem to be very helpful. Things went from bad to worse, especially for Sophia Andreyevna, who often behaved like one demented. The drama of incompatibility between the two old people was thus coming to a climax which to an outsider looks almost incredible. How else could one define this accusation which Tolstoy's wife wrote down on July 5th, 1910? 'As soon as I drew near, Leo

Nikolayevitch turned his back to me and his face to his idol [Chertkov] and began talking again of insanity and suicide and madness, discussing it calmly from all sides and analysing that with particular care and exactitude from the point of view of my present suffering.' And on July 13th: 'Where is their Christianity? Where is their love? And where is their non-resistance? All is falsehood, deception, and cruelty.'

While the whole world was fixing its eyes on Yasnaya Polyana and listening to Tolstoy's words of universal love, Tolstoy's own wife saw, instead of love, only distrust and open antagonism. Her husband apparently had no need of her. And he did not mind showing it. The limit of her despair can again be gauged from the pages of her diary. Thus on August 17th she wrote these frantic lines: 'I will throw everything up and let it be lost. Who will master whom? And to think that this malignant strife has arisen between two people who once loved each other so much! Is it old age, or the influence of outsiders? Sometimes I look at him and it seems to me that he is dead, that all that was alive, good, wise, sympathetic, truthful, and loving, has perished and been killed by the hand of that dry, heartless sectarian Chertkov.' Not less sparing are the lines, hastily jotted down by her on October 12th and 13th. However one-sided, they came from the depth of her heart. One of them was that 'he has exchanged all that was straightforward, pure, truthful, and happy, for what is hidden, impure, false, evil and weak! He suffers very much, but throws all the blame on me. . . . I am so frightened by my husband's anger and shouts directed against me that I fear to talk to him.' She seriously thought of escaping from all that 'Christian' atmosphere by committing suicide. But, as she herself acknowledges, when it came to the test, she was too cowardly to do it. 'I wandered back to the house. I don't even remember how. I did not go in, I was afraid to.'

IV

There was yet another matter which aggravated the situation. The landowner Chertkov, who had never thought of distributing his own wealth among his poorer 'Christian brethren', was most anxious that his teacher Tolstoy should seal his gospel by personal example. True enough, Tolstoy's former estate was no longer in his hands. But there was still the copyright for his books. Why should Tolstoy receive any money for his writings if he regarded money as something immoral and thoroughly anti-Christian? Why not renounce, in a true Christian fashion, the royalties once and for all for the benefit of the poor?

Tolstoy was of course on the side of Chertkov. Tolstoy's wife, however, protested, and in no ambiguous terms. She knew only too well that, instead of going to the poor, her husband's royalties would remain in the publishers' safes and pockets—at the expense of her own numerous children and grandchildren. Through Chertkov's influence Tolstoy had previously (in 1891) renounced his posthumous rights only on his works written after 1881. But now he was urged by the same busybody to renounce the copyright on all his works without exception. Tolstoy was actually supposed to have made, with the connivance of Chertkov and of his own youngest daughter Alexandra, a testament to this effect. Sophia Andreyevna was frantic. Determined to defend the rights of her family, she put up a fight which only made the situation worse. It increased her suspicions, nervousness, and hysteria. As a result, Tolstoy's own peace of mind was so unsettled that on September 24th, 1910 he wrote in his diary: 'They are tearing me to shreds. I often think of escaping far away from all of them.' On October 20th he even discussed with a peasant (M. P. Novikov) from the province of Tula the problem of a secret refuge. A few days later he sent a letter to him with some further inquiries and instructions. The idea of going away seemed to be the only outlet. 'Always the same oppression,' he wrote on October 25th. 'Suspicion and spying, and on my side a sinful wish that she (his wife) would give me occasion to go away. How weak I am! I think about going away.' And the next day: 'It is very hard for me in this madhouse.'

On October 28th Tolstoy actually went away. All that happened during the flight is known to the world. Less known is the fact that when the news was broken to Sophia Andreyevna, she threw herself into the pond, but was rescued. Meanwhile, Tolstoy first went to his sister Maria who was a nun in the convent of Shamardino near Kaluga. Then he continued his journey in the direction of Novo-Cherkask, but caught pneumonia and died at the little railway station of Ostapovo. While the station building was besieged by swarms of reporters, photographers, and even cinema-operators, Tolstoy's wife—beside herself with anguish—arrived. She demanded admission to her dying husband, but the doctors and his saintly followers would not let her see him until he became delirious. They wanted to make sure he would no longer recognize her. And in this they succeeded. Such was the end of that strange marriage which had lasted just over forty-eight years.

XI

Tolstoy and the Revolution

IT is often suggested that Tolstoy's influence on the revolution of 1917 was similar to that of Rousseau's upon the revolution of 1789. This is true only in so far as Tolstoy became an indirect revolutionary force, even though his ideas and ideals had nothing to do either with the character or with the consequences of the Russian cataclysm. His doctrine of non-resistance was anti-revolutionary in its very essence and, as Lenin himself remarked in 1911, played into the hands of the oppressors. Regarding any exercise of power or authority as a dividing agent and therefore immoral, he moreover condemned not only revolutions, but all man-made laws —even when these were concerned with the planning or the working for a better future. He actually ridiculed the idea that we could know or plan anything about the social forms of the future and saw in it a superstition, alongside with such other superstitions as patriotism, science and anti-religious thought. 'When you have freed yourselves from these superstitions', he insists in his article *On Socialism,* 'you should first of all endeavour to study all that which has been attained by the great thinkers of mankind concerning the true basis of life. And when you have thus acquired a sound religious life-conception, you should next endeavour to fulfil its demand not with the object of achieving—by yourselves or by any one else—certain aims, but in order to fulfil the purpose of human life unmistakably leading to an unknown, but blissful destiny.'

We quote this passage on account of its typical contradiction. It advocates the old Tolstoyan 'rules' as to how to live, and at the same time enforces the advice not to plan but to abandon ourselves to an irrational 'unknown but blissful destiny' without bothering whither it leads. Such a shaky precept would land us (if viewed realistically) not even in Tolstoy's 'Christian' anarchism, but in absolute passivity on the one hand, and in the law of the jungle on the other.

Both Rousseau and Tolstoy were rebels, not because they looked forward, but backward to a past stage of consciousness. Their moral revolt against the conditions in which they lived was due to similar although not identical reasons. Rousseau was an ambitious and gifted plebeian with a grudge against those privileged classes which represented the culture of his time and on whose charity he largely depended. Feeling a stranger in that artificial and morally corrupt society, he identified its pattern of life with the whole of civilization and attacked it with all the fury of his social 'inferiority complex'. He exalted the simple and the humble above the privileged. True happiness, morality, and goodness he found not among the mighty, but among the uneducated masses and the 'children of nature'. It was a rebellion from below.

Tolstoy's rebellion was, however, one from above. He saw in civilization not only the chief cause of division among men, but also the affirmation of everything material at the expense of man's spirit and morals. And since his own upper class represented the climax of material comfort derived from the exploited masses, Tolstoy turned against it to the extent of denying its very right to exist. Like Rousseau, he discovered happiness only among the exploited lower strata, although he ascribed it primarily to a low level of consciousness. His mouthpiece Prince Andrey put it rather crudely when remarking to Pierre (who wanted to alleviate the lot of his serfs): 'Why raise the peasant from his animal condition? Animal happiness is the only happiness and you want to deprive him of it. Physical labour is as essential to him, as much a condition of his existence, as mental activity is to me.' A further explanation is to be found in *Three Deaths*, as well as in Tolstoy's entire campaign against individuation and the growth of consciousness.

II

The converted Tolstoy called, of course, that kind of happiness by loftier names. He knew only too well why he himself sought for peace, happiness, and 'brotherhood' not at the top but at the bottom of the social pyramid. His hatred of civilization thus blended not only with his idea of moral self-perfection, but also with his cult of the moujik, which brought him—at least externally—close to the populists.

The Russian populism (whose originator was Alexander Herzen) consisted largely of 'repentant noblemen' anxious to redeem the guilt of their serf-owning ancestors. There was a moral as well as a sentimental impulse in their homage to the Russian peasant. The left wing populists even aimed at a kind of agrarian socialism which would secure—by revolutionary means if necessary—both land and liberty to the peasants and thus perhaps avert the ravages of capitalism from Russia. The movement was at its height in the 'seventies, when numbers of aristocratic youths and girls renounced their privileges and went to work among the masses in order to prepare them for the forthcoming rising. With what meagre results, can best be gathered from Turgenev's novel, *The Virgin Soil*. However much Tolstoy disliked the anti-religious mentality of the radical populists, he not only shared with them the cult of the peasant, but actually demanded that all the land should be given, and unconditionally so, to the people. In this clamour he persisted even long after the wave of populism had subsided.[1]

[1] The so-called social revolutionaries of 1905 and 1915 were the descendants

In the 'eighties again, when—after the assassination of Alexander II—the reaction, triumphant once more, succeeded in frustrating any activities, Tolstoy's other ideal, that of moral self-perfection, was welcomed by many an intellectual as the only refuge from the general blind-alley and stagnation. Chekhov himself was for a while under the influence of Tolstoy—a phase of development which he recorded in his story, *My Life*. But he soon found out that Tolstoyanism itself was a blind-alley and said so (in his short story, *The Gooseberries*, etc.). On the other hand, it was precisely in the 'eighties that Tolstoy's own aggressiveness increased, and this not only in his pamphlets, but also in his narratives and plays. His realism of invectives now took an intolerant moral direction and justification.

There was indeed hardly an evil that escaped Tolstoy's scrutiny. He may have been biased and one-sided, especially in his propensity to over-simplify things so as to make them fit into his own schemes and 'rules'. Yet what mattered in the end was the manner in which he vented his indignation. Ruthless marshalling of facts, irony, would-be *naïveté* of a child puzzled by the unfathomable imbecility of the grown-ups, cumulative stress on the main idea, calculated repetition of certain words—such and similar devices contributed to the final effect not only of his literary works, but also of his pamphlets and essays. The more so because he regarded it as his duty to tear off all masks in order to show the ugly face of reality.

One of his most slashing pamphlets, *Christianity and Patriotism*, can be quoted as an example. Tolstoy wrote it after the conclusion of the Franco-Russian alliance in 1893. The actual pretext was provided, however, by the hysterical patriotic manifestations during a visit of the Russian warships at Toulon. Resisting the 'general tendency' as usual,

of the populists who, in contrast to the Marxians, pinned their faith on the peasants and not on the industrial workers.

Tolstoy chose this occasion in order to deal a blow not only at patriotism, but also at its off-shoot—militarism. And he did it less in terms of direct exhortation than concrete description. This is how he presents his vision of a prospective war:

'The bells will begin ringing, men with long hair[1] will dress up in gold embroidered sacks and begin praying for murder. And the old horrible business familiar for ages will begin over again. The journalists will get to work, egging men on under the guise of patriotism to hatred and murder, and will be delighted at doubling their sales. The factory-owners, the merchants, the purveyors of army stores, will gleefully get to work, expecting doubled profits. Officials of all sorts will get to work, receiving double salary and rations, and hoping to win for murdering men various trinkets greatly prized by them—ribbons, crosses, stripes, stars. The idle ladies and gentlemen will get to work putting their names down for the Red Cross, getting ready to bandage those whom their own husbands or brothers are going to wound, and imagining that in this they are doing a very Christian deed. And drowning the despair in their hearts with singing, debauchery, and vodka, torn away from peaceful labour, from their wives, their mothers, and their children, hundreds of thousands of simple, good-natured men, with weapons of murder in their hands, will trudge off where they are sent. They will march, will be frozen, will be hungry, will be sick, some dying of disease; till at last they reach the place where they will be murdered by thousands, and will themselves, not knowing why, murder thousands of men whom they have never seen, who have done them no wrong. And when the mass of the sick, wounded, and killed is so great that no one can gather them up, and when the air is so contaminated by the rotting cannon-flesh that it becomes unpleasant even for the commanding officer, then they will stop for a time, will

[1] The Russian priests used to wear long hair and long beards.

pick up the wounded after a fashion and carry them off, will throw the sick together in heaps, anywhere that comes first, and will bury the slain in the earth, sprinkling them with lime, and will lead the crowd of their dupes farther, and will go on leading them forward till those who have contrived all the mischief are weary of it, or till those who have something to gain have gained all they want.'

After such passages the realism of which speaks for itself, he feels on safer ground when attacking what he himself regards as the cause of our wars, namely patriotism. Here, too, as elsewhere, he swims against current. And he explains why. 'It is a terrible thing to say,' he continues, 'but there is not, and there never has been a combined act of violence by one set of people upon another set of people which has not been perpetrated in the name of patriotism. In the name of patriotism the Russians have waged war on the French and the French on the Russians. And in the name, too, of patriotism the Russians are now preparing with the French to make war on the Germans, and in the name of patriotism the Germans are preparing now to wage war on two fronts. But it is not only war—in the name of patriotism the Russians oppress the Poles and the Germans the Slavs; in the name of patriotism the Communards slaughtered the Versaillistes and the Versaillistes slaughtered the Communards,' etc., etc. . . .

III

Such was the language Tolstoy dared to use at a time when in Russia, at any rate, the thought and the press were muzzled by the tsarist police. Yet it is not difficult to see once again that his vehemence is due to his simplification of both the problem and the issue. When proclaiming patriotism as the sole cause of wars, Tolstoy is so persuasive that it takes quite a time before the reader comes to himself and begins to question his statement. And even when he has realized that patriotism has little to do with the deeper causes of war, Tolstoy's pictures of war are likely to haunt his mind as well as his moral sense.

But war was only one of Tolstoy's targets. Most of his literary works, written after 1880, are a powerful *j'accuse* of our entire social, mental, and moral heritage. Yet even in his invectives he continued to glorify the exploited peasant masses as the only human material worth while. In *The Death of Ivan Ilyitch* it is the servant Gerasim alone who knows how to alleviate the dying patient's mental and moral agony. The peasants of his *Folk Tales,* such as *Three Old Men* and *What People Live By,* have an ikonographic flavour. And in his posthumous *Alyosha Gorshok* we find a new variety of the Karatayev type, in his simplicity even more naïve and refreshing.

In short, it is not so much the reasoning Tolstoy as Tolstoy the accuser and the artist combined that is likely to kindle one's revolutionary temper. That is why his dry theological writings are the least interesting portion of his work—even from the standpoint of theology. On the other hand, his pictures illustrating the injustice and iniquities of our time will always have due effect, no matter what his private conclusions may be. Who could ever forget his description of the Moscow down-and-outs as he himself had seen them in one of the notorious dosshouses of that city? A competent economist would probably smile at many a statement in such a pamphlet as *The Slavery of Our Time,* but he could hardly help being shocked by the horrors of modern capitalism unbound as described by Tolstoy. And what is even more important, Tolstoy's voice rang fearlessly and recklessly all over Russia at a time when practically all the other voices of protest were silenced by the police and censorship. Whether his indictments were or were not allowed to appear in Russia, mattered little: they circulated in numerous written copies the effect of which was even stronger. Thus in the very heat of the Russo-Japanese War of 1904–5, he launched one of the most anti-militarist pamphlets ever written. And when after the frustrated rising of 1905 the tsarist government indulged in an orgy of daily executions, Tolstoy hurled at the Russian reactionaries a pamphlet more deadly than any political or other demonstrations. And again, it was Tolstoy's art that proved better propaganda than Tolstoy's sermons. What this art was like, can be gathered from the following extract describing the execution of twelve peasants in Kherson, on account of their revolutionary activities.

'Twelve of those by whose labour we live, the very men whom we have depraved and are still depraving by every means in our power—from the poison of vodka to the terrible falsehood of a creed we do not ourselves believe in, but impose on them with all our might—twelve of those men, strangled with cords by those whom they feed and clothe and house, and who have depraved and still continue to deprave them. Twelve husbands, fathers, sons, from among those on whose kindness, industry, and simplicity alone rests the whole of Russian life, were seized, imprisoned, and shackled. Then their hands were tied behind their backs, lest they should seize the ropes by which they would be hung, and they were led to the gallows. Several peasants similar to those who are about to be hung, but armed, dressed in clean soldiers' uniforms, with good boots on their feet, and with guns in their hands, accompany the condemned men. Beside them walks a long-haired man, wearing a stole and vestments of gold and silver cloth, and bearing a cross. The procession stops. The manager of the whole business says something; the secretary reads a paper; and when the paper has been read, the long-haired man, addressing these whom other people are about to strangle with cords, says something about God and Christ. Immediately after these words, the hangmen (there are several, for one man could not manage so complicated a business) dissolve some soap, and having soaped the loops in the cord that they may tighten better, seize the shackled men, put shrouds on them, lead them to a scaffold, and place the well-soaped nooses round their necks. And then, one after another, living men are pushed off the benches which are drawn from under their feet, and by their own weight suddenly tighten the nooses round their necks, and are painfully strangled. Men, alive a minute before, become corpses dangling from a rope; at first slowly swinging, and then resting motionless. . . . A doctor makes his round of the bodies, feels them, and reports to those in authority that the business has been done properly: all twelve are certainly dead. And those in authority depart to their ordinary occupations, with the consciousness of a necessary though painful task performed. The bodies now grow cold, are taken down and buried.'

IV

The curious point about this gruesome picture is that it resembles a child's drawing—with nothing but the essentials. Even the language used is often that of a child. Instead of saying 'the priest', Tolstoy says 'a long-haired man, wearing a stole and vestments of gold and silver cloth'—the details which would strike a child's imagination first. Also the procedure of hanging is described from the standpoint of an observant child. But the shock achieved by such a 'simplifying' method is all the greater. Having stirred up the reader's revolutionary disposition and brought his disgust with the government to a pitch, Tolstoy suddenly turns against the revolutionaries: not so much in order to condemn them as the government. 'You, Government-men,' he thunders, 'call the acts of the revolutionaries "atrocities", and "great crimes", but they have done and are doing nothing you have not done, and done to an incomparably greater extent.'

However much he disapproved of revolution, he always retained a soft spot for the revolutionaries. Whereas Dostoevsky saw in them criminal maniacs (at least as described in his novel, *The Possessed*), Tolstoy treated them in *Resurrection,* for example, with sympathy and respect. He made the prostitute Maslova show the first signs of moral rebirth through her contact with the political convicts, and not with her would-be saviour Nekhlyudov whom she secretly loathed. The women revolutionaries (Vera Yefremovna, Maria Pavlovna, Rantseva) are depicted with particular warmth. And as for their male companions, their high ethical level is above suspicion, even if Simonson's dry-as-dust dogmaticism is neither convincing nor interesting. On the other hand, the idea of non-resistance became Tolstoy's fixed idea, and nothing would make him depart from such an attitude. While thoroughly anti-revolutionary in this respect, he yet fostered—by his art, his indictments, and his moral indignation—all sorts of revolutionary moods and dispositions at a time when the whole of Russia was becoming thoroughly receptive for them.

Through the energies of his fanatical adherent, Vladimir Chertkov, Tolstoy's seditious booklets appeared in cheap popular editions. Peddled all over Russia, they acted as an eye-opener among the readers: from the aristocratic and over-refined intellectuals to the half-literate peasants and factory workers. For reasons of their own, the tsarist police refrained from turning Tolstoy into a martyr. This means that he was allowed to say things for which any other Russian would have had to pay very dearly. Tolstoy took full advantage of such a privilege by criticizing all the more outspokenly the anomalies and iniquities of our time.

It was in this capacity that he became not only a kind of 'conscience of his age', but also a revolutionary stimulus, ominously looming on the horizon of modern Russia. In spite of his negative attitude towards revolutionary activities, he cleared much of the ground for the last revolution which took place only seven years after his death. This is only another of his contradictions. But contradictions were as much a part of his complexity as the latter was a part of his greatness. And greatness is frequently the heaviest of burdens.

XII

Tolstoy and Nietzsche

TOLSTOY's urge to simplify everything, including himself, came largely from fear of his own inner complexity. But if this be so, it is all the more tempting to approach Tolstoy the artist and the moralist through Tolstoy the man—especially in the light of some of our present-day needs and tasks. His work as a whole, sifted through the drama of his personality, thus acquires an additional facet. And the interest of it may be all the greater when confronted with the work and personality of his younger contemporary and antipodes, Friedrich Nietzsche. Having tackled a very similar inner cleavage, but in the opposite direction, Nietzsche may clarify quite a few aspects of Tolstoy from the other end. The more so because Tolstoy and Nietzsche were children of the same disintegrating age—an age which both of them repudiated with the same vehemence, although their aims and ideals were utterly incompatible. And finally, both of them not only tried to give their own personal dilemmas a universal significance, but actually found a wide echo for the very reason that they tackled certain problems inherent in the present-day consciousness, and therefore demanding an answer from each of us.

As moralists, seekers and artists in one, Tolstoy and Nietzsche produced works didactic in character yet of great literary value. *Thus Spake Zarathustra* may be infinitely more stimulating in this respect than Tolstoy's *Resurrection,* for instance, but Nietzche was always at his best as a thinker, whereas Tolstoy could not help showing his one-track mind outside the realm of artistic creation proper. All-embracing and truly universal as an artist, he cuts a somewhat poor figure beside the wealth of Nietzsche's explosive thoughts and ideas. In fact, from Olenin's 'discovery' in *The Cossacks* that the only possible happiness is to live for others, and until his last days, Tolstoy the thinker remained a man of one idea, the endless variations of which would be tedious if they were expressed in a less attractive form. There can be no doubt that, by temperament, Nietzsche was more of a visionary and a prophet than Tolstoy. Yet the intensity of his anti-Christian trend was due, in the last resort, to the same one-sidedness and method of exclusion which was responsible for the 'Christian' and puritan trend of Tolstoy.

It is, of course, easy to decry Nietzsche as a madman and to put to his charge even such an abortion of human mind and nature as the Nazi doctrine. But what has the essential and true Nietzsche to do with the vulgarized or deliberately distorted Nietzscheanism? Besides, was it not he who had warned us beforehand against his own 'apes', coming from the intellectual and moral gutter? Even those who still see in Nietzsche an apostle of the zoological brand of German nationalism are inclined to forget that no other German of note—with the exception of Hoelderlin in his *Hyperion*—had ever said more cruel things about the Germans than Nietzsche. It was he who saw in his country's triumph over France in 1871 a cultural defeat of Germany and was full of pessimistic forebodings. Precisely because he knew so well who and what the Germans were, did he spend most of his mature life outside Germany. He also prided himself on his Polish origin, obviously to spite his own thick-skinned compatriots. In his will to surpass the present-day man, he was anxious above all to surpass the Prussianized German in whom he rightly sensed one of the greatest dangers to any culture—let alone that higher type of culture for which he himself was striving.

Be this as it may, both Nietzsche and Tolstoy had personal reasons for most of the problems they tackled, and particularly for their negations which, in the end, comprised all the aspects of contemporary life. As children of a sceptical and one-sidedly scientific age, which had undermined all the old values of life without having replaced them by any new ones, they witnessed the process of an entire civilization on the eve of the crumbling away to its doom. And the fact that the remedies offered by them were at the opposite poles, is itself typical of the consciousness of that age.

II

The very starting-point of their inquiry is one of the crucial problems of mankind: the problem of the individual self. And is it not significant that whereas Tolstoy arrived at an absolute negation of the individual, Nietzsche exalted the individual principle to the point of divinity? Yet he drew a sharp line between individualism and egoism—a distinction which Tolstoy never cared to make, although there is a point where the two can even exclude each other. It was the quality of the species that mattered to Nietzsche, and his entire sociology was but a quest for conditions able to produce and to maintain not only the highest biological type of man, but also what he regarded as the noblest representative of mankind. Whether rightly or wrongly, he proclaimed 'will to power' on the one hand, and a continuous dynamic struggle—not for its own sake, but in the name of a creative goal—as the two factors disciplining those individuals who grow strong through difficulties encountered and overcome. Conflict, diversity of interests, inequality and differentiation represented for him the very basis of that intense and vigorous life which would direct one's will beyond contemporary humanity. His nightmare was the mere quantitative element as the ruler of the world. Consequently, he was all the more anxious to devise a pattern of existence, based on an order of rank the root-idea of which was that quantity should exist for the sake of quality, and not vice versa.

Nietzsche—himself a product of a capitalist civilization—was right in regarding the quantitative principle as typical of our commercialized bourgeois era. But he was wrong in connecting it necessarily with democracy. For one thing, he was never able to distinguish between democracy and plebeianism with its levelling down tendency. Having turned against the whole of the modern democratic movement, he thus cut himself off from the only modern current which might perhaps still be susceptible to true creative influences and thus alter the pattern of our life in a desirable direction. He was thrown back upon himself and, in his isolation, felt entirely 'out of season' (*unzeitgemaess*), while choking with disgust, with self-protective spite, and with terrible forebodings about the future. His dream of an *élite* of supermen as masters of the many was but a romantic shelter in which he barricaded himself against the vulgarity of our capitalism triumphant. And the more he suffered from it, the more glowing became his dream which he embodied in symbols, reminiscent of the visions of ancient prophets and makers of myths. His Zarathustra is in fact the nearest modern equivalent of both. Unfortunately, he identified himself too much with that symbol and, in his personal inflation, began to look upon the whole of humanity as raw material to be shaped by him according to his own ideal which was beyond pity, as it was beyond good and evil in our sense. His love was intended only for the far ones to come. And such love demanded hardness—creative hardness towards one's 'neighbours' and even more towards oneself.

Reverse all this, and you will obtain the ideal of Tolstoy who appreciated personality only in so far as it sacrificed itself to the many and to the compactness of the many. The individual self-affirmation, so ardently preached by Nietzsche, was in Tolstoy's eyes the original sin of man and therefore the spring of all the evil on earth. Nietzsche discarded God with hysterical vehemence in order to procure to the individual the unlimitable freedom of man-God. Tolstoy, on the other hand, shaped his own idea of divinity in such a way as to find in it the embodiment and the ultimate sanction of self-effacement. Seeing in our usual forms of 'selflessness' only masked egoism and weakness, Nietzsche was frank about it and never missed an opportunity of jeering at their pious disguises. He maintained that since, anyway, there was no God there could be no transcendental scale of values, obligatory for all men. But while thus advocating complete relativity of morals, he also taught that the value of an action depends on the inherent worth and value of the individual who performs it. Only those who are noble in themselves can act nobly. An ignoble person may put on all the private and public virtues, yet he will debase them to his own level, no matter how 'respectable' or even Christian they look on the surface.

According to Tolstoy, man in his individual separateness has no right to exist. Consequently, his actions can only be measured by their conformity to the universal moral categories, obligatory for all men and all times. It was Tolstoy's stern, 'Thou shalt', that Nietzsche counteracted with his, 'I will', on a plane of beyond good and evil as far as our old moral valuations are concerned. To will extra-morally and supra-morally should be, however, a privilege of those few only who are strong and *moral* enough for it; who are capable of imposing the highest possible meaning upon a meaningless world. Otherwise the slogan of 'beyond good and evil' would serve only as a gateway to profligacy, moral nihilism, and universal chaos.

Whereas Tolstoy's valuations were of the strictest puritan order, the valuations of Nietzsche were above all those of taste. Tolstoy preached a community of meek and selfless men united in that static pre-individual love in which alone he saw a guarantee for peace and happiness. Nietzsche, on the contrary, turned human fate into a drama and demanded from his supermen a continuous creative and self-creative effort, accompanied by a spiteful laughter at all 'easy yokes'. He extolled that beautifully tragic courage which makes a hard and dangerous life a duty. At the same time he wanted our virtues, and especially our goodness, to grow not out of fear and cowardice (as is so often the case), but out of our surplus of strength. The meanness and frustration posing as goodness should be replaced by the free, generous, and 'bestowing' virtue (*schenkende Tugend*) of the future. Nietzsche—at least the Nietzsche of *Thus Spake Zarathustra* —here compares with the preaching Tolstoy as a mountain-top compares with a prison.

III

The irony of it all was that the Utopia of both Tolstoy and Nietzsche, while reflecting their inner conflicts, served also as an escape from reality, and especially from themselves. We know that Tolstoy kept on stressing his own 'Christianity' because he was anxious to suppress the latent pagan within himself. But curiously enough, it was his pagan fear of death that became the chief spring of his subsequent 'Christian' conversion. Endowed with an exclusively rich and self-assertive personality, he yet preached the abolition of the personal self, in order to get rid of those painful inner conflicts which are perhaps the very condition of its growth. And by doing this, he threatened life itself with a kind of ossification, i.e. with the narrowing it down to the fulfilment of a few moral 'rules'.

Nietzsche's dilemma was the other way round. Whereas the young pagan Tolstoy indulged in physical excesses, Nietzsche knew only the excesses of the intellect and spirit which he took, however, with deadly seriousness. But no sooner had he been afflicted with his infirmity than he began to glorify the biological man—later on even in the shape of the *bestia bionda*—at the expense of his over-developed spirit. In essence, his very praise of the body was a mental act designed to supply new vitality to his own decaying physique. As he once said, he was a decadent, determined to cure himself by his own opposite. And his chief medicament was his philosophy. So he exalted that very body which the converted Tolstoy tried to despise or—as he put it—to turn into an 'obedient dog of the spirit'. Nietzsche crucified his spirit on his flesh, and Tolstoy his flesh on his spirit. Yet neither of them succeeded, because their very method (the method of suppression) was wrong. As if realizing this, they both insisted all the more that they were what they wished and professed to be. Tolstoy, with his instincts of an intensified pagan, did all he could to prove that he was a Christian, only a Christian. Nietzsche, on the other hand, who, by his temperament and inclinations, was a latent Christian of the highest order, wrote some of the most cruel invectives against Christianity—in order to convince himself and the world that he was the fiercest anti-Christian ever born.

As a semi-invalid, Nietzsche probably realized that Christianity, with its cult of resignation, might perhaps bring him solace and comfort. But this itself was only a further reason why he rejected it. Had he even been a believer, his pride would never have allowed him to 'wag his tail' before God at a moment when he needed Him as a shelter from his own suffering. With a disposition such as this, he was bound to discard any philandering with religions and philosophies of comfort as something unmanly or even indecent. On the other hand, his very recklessness gave him an illusion of increased vitality. It transmuted his suffering into a feeling of power and of defiant 'joy'.

Viewed in this light, Nietzsche's Promethean struggle with

Fate was certainly more heroic than Tolstoy's non-resistance with its craving for 'good pastures' and other advantages. Nietzsche's 'artifice of self-preservation' may have been full of emergency shelters, masks, and evasions. But he availed himself of these as a kind of strategic ruse which, instead of eliminating his fight, ought to help him to win it in the end. While Nietzsche was compelled to face his inner conflicts even in their worst implications, Tolstoy hurried to barricade himself behind his own version of Christianity as a kind of 'bottom from which there is no place to fall'. What he called God's will was primarily a pretext for condemning one's personal will and personal self. The peace he aimed at was the peace of self-obliteration, of living death. And this at a time when Nietzsche's *Zarathustra* preached creative self-realization as the first duty of man, regardless whether such a path should lead towards happiness or pain.

IV

Peace and 'good pastures' in Tolstoy's sense were considered by Nietzsche as the depth of decadence. So was the morality underlying them. Yet Nietzsche's own moral urge was at least as strong as that of Tolstoy. And the fact that it was a refutation of everything which Tolstoy's 'Categorical Imperative' stands for is itself a sign of the crisis through which the moral and the Christian consciousness of our time is passing. Is it not surprising that Nietzsche turned against contemporary Christianity from an excess of that Christian integrity which he found in himself, but not in the Christians of our time? 'The Christianity of my forebears,' he says, 'reaches its logical conclusion in me: a stern intellectual conscience, fostered and made by Christianity itself, turns against Christianity; in me Christianity raises itself and overcomes itself.' Compared with this, Tolstoy's Christianity seems devoid of true substance. A strange mixture of his archaic *daimonion* on the one hand and of his moralizing rationalism on the other, it points, and most decidedly so, not to Christ, but to the piously camouflaged Eastern nihilism with its negation of culture and its hidden longing for the Nirvana.

However much Tolstoy and Nietzsche may exclude each other, they are yet complementary—as the two opposite poles—in a quest which concerns not only them, but all of us. At the same time they share the same mistake, since both of them tried to cope with their conflicts not through integration, but through suppression. Hence in both cases the result was something distorted and hostile to life. Nietzsche's inflated self eventually led him to rancorous megalomania and madness. Tolstoy, on the other hand, was landed in Christian and humanitarian sentimentality as well as in that kind of puritanism which is likely to degenerate into the most vicious negation of life—vicious from too much virtue.

Their value for us resides above all in their creative elements. Tolstoy's art and sense of life is one of them. Nietzsche's Dionysian verve, full of stimulating intuitions, but utterly untenable as a 'system' is the other. Otherwise they are important mainly as warnings. The path towards life, towards a complete and full existence, points to a plane which, in this respect, is beyond both Tolstoy and Nietzsche.

Conclusion

AUTHORS of Tolstoy's calibre usually call for a certain adjustment on the part of each successive generation. All that is truly creative in them becomes enhanced by such a process, while the negative elements are shown by it in their proper perspective. Tolstoy the artist has nothing to fear from revisions of this kind—he will survive them all. Tolstoy the 'prophet' may be a different matter. But even so there remains the intense personality of Tolstoy which will always present a fascinating study: partly on account of the contradictions and complications which he had failed to master, and partly because his personality provides the best clue to his literary genius which, after all, is the main thing.

Those who consider him a new apostle or even a saint, misunderstand him at the very outset. For one thing, his tragedy of seeking and suffering is of greater importance than all his saintly masks. And secondly, he himself warned us against pious misconceptions of his personality in a passage (written in 1892) with which we can conclude our present study.

'I am no saint, and I have never given myself out for a saint,' he insists; 'I am a man liable to be carried away, and sometimes, or, more correctly, always, I say not fully what I think and feel: not because I do not wish to say it, but because I am unable to, I frequently exaggerate, and often simply err.

'This refers to words. As regards acts, it is even worse.

'I am an absolutely weak man, with vicious habits, who

wishes to serve the God of truth, but who constantly misses the road.

'The moment I am looked upon as a man who cannot err, every mistake of mine appears either as a lie or as hypocrisy.

'But if I am understood to be a weak man, the disagreement between my words and my acts will be a sign of weakness, and not of lying and hypocrisy. And then I shall appear as what I really am: bad, but sincerely, with my whole soul, always and even now, wishing to be absolutely good, that is, a good servant of God.'

Index

Alexander I, 27, 29
Alexander II, 146
Auerbach, B., 11, 12

Balou, Adin, 113
Beethoven, 78
Behrs, C. A., 104
Behrs, S. A. (subsequently Tolstoy's wife), 13, 120
Behrs, Tanya (Tatyana), 133
Belinsky, 19
Bestuzhev-Marlinsky, 39
Biryukov, P., 11
Byron, 19

Chekhov, 146
Chertkov, V., 130, 136, 137, 138, 139, 140, 152
Chicherin, 12
Crosby, E. H., 113

Dante, 116
Dostoevsky, 9, 12, 20, 34, 73, 97, 111, 151

Eikhenbaum, K., 29

Fet, A. A., 9, 65, 76, 82, 85, 88

Garshin, 62
Gay, N. N., 127
Gandhi, 79
Genghis Khan, 108
Goethe, 78
Gogol, 19
Goldenveizer, 77, 98
Gorky, 16, 65, 117
Gotthelf, J., 12
Grigorovitch, 9, 11, 12, 20

Hartung (Baroness), 33
Herzen, 11, 12, 145
Hoelderlin, 154

Ivanov-Razumnik, 29

Kant, 107
Kutuzov, 74

Lenin, 143
Leontyev, 31
Lermontov, 19, 39
Lichtenberg, 77

de Maistre, Joseph, 29
Maude, Aylmer, 65, 133

Napoleon, 13, 27, 29, 71, 73, 88
Nekrasov, 10
Nicholas I, 13
Nietzsche, 153–161

Pascal, 101
Pogodin, Prof., 29
Proudhon, 11, 27, 29
Pushkin, 19, 33, 39, 78

Rousseau, 12, 13, 20, 67, 90, 101, 143, 144
Rubinstein, Anton, 65

Schelling, 29
Seuron, Anna, 79
Shakespeare, 78
Shelgunov, 74
Shklovsky, 29
Socrates, 107
Sophia Andreyevna. *See* Tolstaya, S. A. (Tolstoy's wife)

Stendhal, 22
Sterne, 20
Strakhov, 95
Styka, Jan, 97

Tolstaya, Alexandra (Tolstoy's distant relative and friend), 5, 84, 94
Tolstaya, Alexandra Lvovna (Tolstoy's daughter), 133, 136
Tolstaya, Maria (Tolstoy's sister), 142
Tolstaya, Sophia Andreyevna (Tolstoy's wife), 121, 122, 123, 124, 126, 131–142
Tolstoy, Leo Lvovitch (Tolstoy's son), 127
Tolstoy, Nicholas (Tolstoy's brother), 85
Turgenev, 9, 10, 15, 19, 20, 37, 65, 79, 145

Urusov, S. S. (Prince), 29

Yergolskaya, Tatyana, 2